menű

Brigitte Dolman

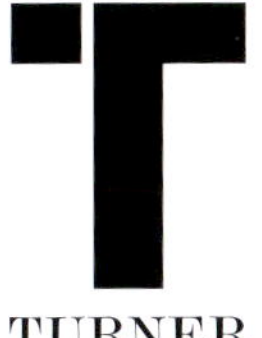

Content

PREFACE

For as long as I can remember, gastronomy has been my greatest passion. Not just for the act of cooking itself, but for everything that surrounds it: a love of detail, and the pursuit of harmony, beauty, and perfection. This sensitivity was passed down through my French roots and deepened with every experience and every lesson, and, above all, through a profound admiration for those who have devoted their lives to the culinary arts.

For many years, that passion took shape in a deeply personal culinary project: Escuela Collectania, which I directed in Caracas since 2003. There, I had the privilege of welcoming great chefs, both international and Venezuelan, who shared their knowledge, technique, and vision with generosity. Names like Santi Santamaria, Claude Troisgros, Thierry Breton, Thierry Mugnier, Carlo Lazzaron, Carlos García, David Posner, and Enrique Limardo—among many others—left a mark not only on my cooking, but also on how I understand this craft. This book was born of that admiration, of gratitude, and of a desire to reinterpret what I've learned through my own lens.

Menú is my way of paying tribute to all that learning. It is a collection of personal interpretations—recipes rooted in tradition, but adapted to my style and to the kind of cooking that defines me: sober, clean, contemporary, centered on respect for the product and on the aesthetics of the plate. Each menu includes at least one appetizer, one main course, and one dessert, designed to be prepared as a complete meal or mixed and matched to suit your taste and the occasion.

Writing this book has been a long and demanding process: gathering recipes, rewriting them, researching, editing, testing them again and again—until finally seeing them photographed just as I had envisioned. Each recipe is accompanied by a personal note in which I explain its essence or share a detail that makes it unique. Each menu also mentions the chef who inspired it, along with their background and story—because behind every dish, there are people, moments, memories. And that is what I hope to convey.

This book does not seek complexity, but clarity. It does not strive for extravagance, but for the elegance found in simplicity. It champions versatility, quality ingredients, and a modern approach that honors tradition while embracing reinvention. I want this to be a useful book—real, repeatable, with that little spark of grace that makes a dish truly shine.

There is immense joy behind every page: the joy of sharing, of breaking with the habit of keeping recipes secret. ***Menú*** is my way of reaching out to you from my kitchen, from my story, from what I love most.

But what gives this book its true meaning is the love of my family—my rock, my daily inspiration. My husband Claudio has been my unwavering pillar. His support, his patience, his unshakable belief in me and my dreams… Thank you for always being there, with your boundless love. My daughter Nicole played a vital role in this project: her talent, her sensitivity, and her professional vision helped bring this book to life. And my sons Eric and Patrick, my official tasters and most honest critics, were there for every recipe, from the first bite to the final detail. To my grandchildren—Henry, Paul, and the little princess on her way—thank you for inspiring in me the purest kind of love and giving me even more reasons to cook with joy. What greater happiness than cooking for you!

To my parents, for planting in me the seed of all things French—good wine, good food. It was part of who we were. That is where it all began.

I also thank the entire team who joined me on this journey: Raúl, Juanita, Julio, Miryana, Gabriel—my assistants—and Laura E., Laura B., Leonardo, and Enol—the editorial team—for believing in me from day one. Thank you for putting heart and soul into every page.

And to you, dear reader, who are now opening these pages: I hope you find more than recipes here. I hope you feel the passion, dedication, and love behind each one. May you cook them, make them your own, and share them—for this book was made with love. And with love—as we all know—everything tastes better.

350

Recipes

- Bouillabaisse, *Fruits de Mer, Tuile au Rouille*
- Lobster Medallions, Quinoa Tabbouleh, *Sauce Vierge*
- Scallops *aux Noisettes*, Courgettes, Orange Sauce
- Soufflé *au Grand Marnier*

Chef Thierry Breton

Thierry Breton, the French chef celebrated for his fresh take on classic French cooking, has left his mark on the culinary scene with acclaimed restaurants like Chez Michel, Chez Casimir, and La Pointe du Grouin. Drawing on a background in prestigious French kitchens, he is regarded as the creator of "bistronomy", a blend of bistro charm and haute cuisine. Beyond his talents in the kitchen, Breton has authored several books on French cooking, solidifying his standing in the culinary sphere and earning widespread praise and recognition.

Bouillabaisse, *Fruits de Mer, Tuile au Rouille*

While this recipe was not part of the original menu, a soup is always welcome, and chef Thierry Breton is renowned for his fish soups. For this dish, I selected a bouillabaisse, a signature of Provençal French cuisine. More than just a dish, it is a culinary journey that embodies the history and traditions of the Mediterranean. This dish is made with fish and seafood that give it depth, along with a flavorful fish stock that provides the characteristic bouillabaisse flavor. It is also served with the classic *rouille*, a mildly spicy red sauce. In this version, I included a *tuile* for a bit of contemporary flair.

4 servings

INGREDIENTS

Fish and Shellfish

- 4 skin-on red snapper fillets
- 4 large prawns
- 4 squids

Fish Stock

- 4½ lb. (2 kg) snapper carcasses and heads
- 4 qt. + 1 c. (4 l) water
- 2 bay leaves
- 2 garlic cloves
- ¾ c. (100 g) onion
- ¾ c. (100 g) celery
- ¾ c. (100 g) carrot

Bouillabaisse

- 10½ oz. (300 g) prawn shells
- ¾ c. (200 ml) Pernod
- ⅓ c. + 1 tbsp. (100 ml) white wine
- 1 qt. (1 l) fish stock
- Pinch of saffron
- ⅓ c. + 1 tbsp. (100 ml) olive oil
- ¾ c. (100 g) onion
- ¾ c. (100 g) celery
- ¾ c. (100 g) carrot
- ¾ c. (100 g) fennel
- ¼ c. + 2 tbsp. (80 g) tomato paste

Rouille

- 1 garlic clove
- 3 tbsp. + 1 tsp. (50 ml) white wine vinegar
- Pinch of saffron
- 1 egg
- 1 egg yolk
- 1 tbsp. mustard
- 1 anchovy fillet
- ¾ c. + 1 tbsp. (200 ml) olive oil
- 2 tbsp. + 2 tsp. (40 ml) lemon juice
- Salt

Carrot *Tuile*

- 7 tbsp. (100 g) butter
- 1 c. (120 g) flour
- 3 egg whites (100 g)
- 1 tbsp. + 1 tsp. (20 ml) carrot juice
- Pinch of salt

Miscellaneous

- 1 baguette
- Olive oil

Garnish

- Microgreens
- Edible flowers

PREPARATION

Fish Stock

Chop the fish carcasses and heads into small chunks.
Rinse well.
In a large pot, sauté the garlic, onion, celery, and carrot in olive oil for 5 minutes.
Add the fish parts and stir well.
Add water until the ingredients are completely covered.
Add the bay leaves.
Bring to a boil, regularly skimming off any foam or scum.
Reduce the heat to medium-low and simmer for 20 minutes.

Bouillabaisse

Heat 3 tablespoons (50 ml) olive oil in a saucepan.
Sauté prawn heads and shells over high heat.
Stir in the tomato paste, white wine, and Pernod. Let it reduce by half.
In a separate pan, heat the remaining 3 tablespoons (50 ml) of olive oil.
Gently sauté the onion, carrot, celery, and fennel.
Combine the sautéed vegetables with the heads and shells, the fish stock and saffron.
Simmer over medium-low heat for 30 minutes or until the flavor becomes more concentrated.
Purée the entire mixture, shells and all.

Bouillabaisse, *Fruits de Mer, Tuile au Rouille*

Strain and discard all solids.

Strain again through a fine-mesh sieve to achieve a smooth, velvety texture.

Season to taste and set aside.

Rouille

Heat the garlic, vinegar, and saffron in a small frying pan.

Let it reduce by half.

Add the whole egg, egg yolk, mustard, anchovy, and reduced vinegar mixture to a blender.

Process until smooth.

While blending, slowly pour in the oil until the mixture emulsifies into a mayonnaise-like consistency.

Set aside.

Carrot *Tuile*

Combine all the ingredients.

Place the mixture in a silicone mold for *tuiles* and bake at 350 °F (175 °C) for 5 minutes, or until golden and easily detachable.

Gently remove them from the mold to prevent cracking.

Set aside.

Miscellaneous

Thinly slice the baguette. Arrange on a baking sheet and drizzle with olive oil.

Place another sheet on top to keep the slices flat and bake at 280 °F (140 °C) for 10 minutes, or until golden brown.

Remove when crisp and golden and set aside.

Fish and Shellfish

In a frying pan, sauté the snapper fillets skin-side down.

Repeat the process with the whole prawns and squid sliced into thin rings.

Set aside.

Plating

Pour the hot bouillabaisse into a preheated bowl.

On one side, arrange a small piece of snapper, a prawn, and several squid rings.

Finish by adding a thin toasted baguette slice or a savory *tuile* with a few dots of *rouille*.

Garnish with microgreens and edible flowers, and serve immediately.

Lobster Medallions, Quinoa Tabbouleh, *Sauce Vierge*

In this recipe, I chose to substitute wheat with quinoa, a grain that is easy to prepare and gives this tabbouleh a light, airy texture with a delicious nutty flavor. To dress the quinoa, I used a version of *Sauce Vierge*, created in 1976 by Michel Guérard, a pioneer of nouvelle cuisine, celebrated for its delicate, lighter style. *Sauce Vierge* is traditionally made with olive oil, lemon, salt, and pepper, and may also contain herbs, making it a fresh, light vinaigrette that enhances the flavor of the ingredients in this dish, celebrating its simplicity.

4 servings

INGREDIENTS

Lobster
- 2 lobster tails, approximately 1 lb. (500 g) each

Quinoa Tabbouleh
- ¾ c. (160 g) quinoa (uncooked)
- ⅞ c. (120 g) cucumber
- ⅞ c. (120 g) tomato
- ½ c. (60 g) avocado
- Olive oil
- Lemon
- Salt
- Black pepper

Tapenade
- 10 pitted black olives
- 4 salted anchovy fillets
- Olive oil

PREPARATION

Lobster

Boil the lobster tail for 6 to 8 minutes, depending on the size.

To ensure the tail stays straight, slide a metal spoon along the inside curve of the uncooked lobster.

Once cooked, remove the lobster tail from its shell.

Depending on the desired presentation, it can be left whole or sliced into thin medallions about ⅛ inch (3 mm) thick. Set aside.

Quinoa Tabbouleh

Boil the quinoa in lightly salted water for several minutes, until the water is absorbed and the quinoa is cooked through. Set aside.

Cut the tomatoes, cucumber, and avocado into roughly ¼-inch (4 mm) dice.

Combine with the quinoa.

Make a vinaigrette using olive oil, lemon to taste, salt, and pepper.

Pour over the quinoa mixture and toss to combine.

Reserve a small amount of vinaigrette to add just before serving. Set aside.

Tapenade

Purée 10 pitted olives with 4 salted anchovies and a drizzle of olive oil.

Plating

Take a large plate and place a ring mold in the center.

Spoon the quinoa mixture into the mold halfway, and then gently lift it off.

Arrange the lobster tail or sliced medallions over the quinoa base.

With the help of a squeeze bottle or piping bag, add small dots of tapenade around the dish.

Drizzle with vinaigrette. Serve.

Scallops *aux Noisettes*, Courgettes, Orange Sauce

Unlike the original recipe, I used large U10 scallops rather than smaller ones in this version. Larger scallops are easier to cook, particularly when seared or sautéed, because they withstand the heat without overcooking. I also opted for very thin courgette slices instead of endives, which can have a slightly bitter taste. In this dish, the delicate scallops paired with the tender texture and mild flavor of the courgette, along with the citrusy, mildly acidic orange sauce, create a balance between the sweet and savory notes.

4 servings

INGREDIENTS

Scallops *aux Noisettes*

- 16 U10 scallops (4 per person)
- ½ c. + 1 tbsp. (120 g) high-quality salted butter
- ⅔ c. (80 g) hazelnuts or walnuts
- 2 tbsp. (10 g) parsley, chopped
- Salt
- Black pepper

Courgettes

- 2 courgettes (zucchini)
- 3 tbsp. (40 g) butter

Sauce

- Juice of 6 oranges
- 1 tbsp. (15 g) sugar

PREPARATION

Courgettes

Slice the courgettes lengthwise with a mandoline into very thin slices (1⁄12 inch / 2 mm).

Melt one tablespoon of butter in a frying pan.

Gently sauté the courgette slices for a few minutes until lightly browned on both sides.

Remove from the pan and set aside.

Sauce

In the same pan, heat the sugar until it melts and turns a light caramel color.

Add the orange juice and let it reduce over medium heat for about 8 minutes, until the sauce thickens and darkens in color.

Remove from burner and set aside.

Scallops

Thoroughly dry the scallops using paper towels.

In a separate frying pan, sear the scallops in butter over high heat until browned on both sides.

Remove from the pan and set aside.

In the same pan, add the chopped hazelnuts or walnuts along with the finely chopped parsley.

Sauté for a few minutes until golden.

Remove from the pan and set aside.

Plating

Arrange three slices of courgette on a preheated plate.

Trim the edges to form a rectangular shape.

Arrange the scallops on top of the courgette and drizzle with the hot orange sauce.

Sprinkle with hazelnuts or walnuts and chopped parsley. Garnish and serve immediately.

Soufflé *au Grand Marnier*

It is undeniable—few things are as quintessentially French as a soufflé, particularly when it's flavored with Grand Marnier. The liqueur not only lends a unique touch, but also infuses the soufflé with a sweet, citrussy aroma. To add another layer of texture, I've included a *tuile dentelle*—a light, delicate almond wafer that also adds visual elegance to the dish. Though soufflés require a particular skill, once mastered, it becomes a true delight for both chef and diner.

4 servings

INGREDIENTS

Soufflé

- 2 egg yolks (40 g)
- ¼ c. + 1 tbsp. (60 g) sugar
- ⅓ c. (40 g) all-purpose flour
- 1¼ c. (300 ml) milk
- 10 egg whites (300 g)
- 1 tbsp. + 1 tsp. (20 ml) Grand Marnier
- Powdered sugar (for dusting)

Tuile Dentelle

- 1 c. (125 g) almonds
- 1¼ c. (250 g) sugar
- ½ c. (60 g) flour
- ⅓ c. + 1 tbsp. (100 ml) orange juice
- ½ c. + 1 tbsp. (125 g) butter
- Orange zest
- Lemon zest

For the Molds

- Butter
- Sugar

PREPARATION

Tuile Dentelle

Finely chop the almonds.

Combine all ingredients and chill for a minimum of 3 hours.

Using a silicone baking mat, form circles the size of the soufflé mold and bake at 350 °F (175 °C) until golden.

Remove immediately and let cool.

Store in an airtight container.

Soufflé

Whisk the egg yolks with 2 teaspoons (10 g) of sugar until the mixture becomes pale.

Add the flour.

Heat the milk in a saucepan until it starts boiling.

Gradually add the boiling milk to the egg yolk and sugar mixture.

Heat the mixture for 3 more minutes until thickened.

Allow to cool briefly, then stir in the Grand Marnier.

Separately, whip the egg whites with the remaining sugar until soft peaks form.

Carefully fold the whites into the yolk mixture, beginning with one-third, then folding in the remainder gently.

Transfer the mixture to a piping bag and set aside.

Brush the inside of small soufflé molds from bottom to top with melted butter to aid rising.

Dust with sugar and shake off the excess.

Fill the molds and smooth the tops with a spatula.

Wipe the edges of the molds carefully with your fingertip.

Bake at 375 °F (190 °C) until the soufflé mixture rises and turns golden (about 10 minutes).

Plating

Dust with powdered sugar.

Place a *tuile* on top of each soufflé.

Set the mold on a plate and serve immediately.

m2

- Creamy Sunchoke Soup
- Mussels Marinated with Tarragon
- Scallops with Pistachio, Soy and Balsamic Sauce
- Tiramisu Bonbon

Chef Franz Conde

Venezuelan chef Franz Conde boasts a long-standing culinary career, both in his native country and throughout Europe, where he earned recognition as one of its leading chefs. He is currently the Executive Chef at the Hilton in Amsterdam, where he resides. His career includes roles at the Çırağan Palace Kempinski in Istanbul—then regarded as Turkey's finest hotel—Roberto's in the Netherlands, and his own restaurant, Aragua, in England. In addition, he was Executive Chef at the Athenee Palace Hilton in Bucharest and interned at top Italian restaurants such as Aimo e Nadia, Antica Osteria del Ponte, Enoteca Pinchiorri, and San Domenico.

Creamy Sunchoke Soup

This cream soup has a distinctive and delicate flavor. The sunchoke, or Jerusalem artichoke, is a tuber similar to a potato. Its flavor is similar to an artichoke, with a slightly sweet, nutty note. If not available, substitute with a mix of potatoes and artichokes in equal parts—the result is also delicious. This is a creamy, velvety soup, rich in flavor and perfect for cold days.

4-6 servings

INGREDIENTS

Creamy Sunchoke Soup

- 2 lb. 3 oz. (1 kg) sunchoke (or, alternatively, equal parts potatoes and artichokes)
- 1¼ c. (180 g) onion
- ½ c. (70 g) celery
- ½ c. (70 g) carrot
- ½ c. (70 g) leek
- 4¼–6⅓ c. (1–1.5 l) chicken broth
- 1 bouquet garni of cilantro, parsley, and mint
- ⅓ c. + 1 tbsp. (100 ml) heavy cream
- 1 c. + 2 tbsp. (250 g) butter

Garnish

- 2 sunchokes or artichokes
- Butter
- Salt
- Edible flowers
- Olive oil

PREPARATION

Creamy Sunchoke Soup

Chop the vegetables and cook in chicken stock until soft.

Blend until smooth and strain.

Reheat, stir in the heavy cream, and simmer gently.

Add the butter and the bouquet garni for flavor.

Remove the bouquet garni before serving.

Garnish

Peel the sunchokes and place in lemon water to keep from browning.

Slice or dice them, season with salt, and sauté in butter.

Set aside.

Plating

Ladle the soup into warm bowls.

Garnish with a few slices of sautéed sunchoke or artichoke and edible flowers.

Drizzle with a few drops of olive oil for a glossy finish.

Serve immediately.

Mussels Marinated with Tarragon

This is a simple, flavorful, and light dish—ideal as a cold appetizer or starter. It is a delicious blend of textures and flavors. The perfectly cooked mussels pair nicely with the fresh, creamy mayonnaise, avocado, and tarragon sauce. The sherry vinegar gives it a refined tartness and elegant finish that perfectly balances the richness of the sauce.

6-8 servings

INGREDIENTS

Mussels
- 4½ lb. (2 kg) mussels, live and cleaned
- ⅔ c. (150 ml) white wine
- 3½ oz. (100 g) fresh parsley
- 1⅓ c. (200 g) chopped onion
- 2 tbsp. (30 g) butter

Mayonnaise
- 1 egg
- 1 tbsp. + 1 tsp. (20 g) Dijon mustard
- 1 tbsp. (15 ml) lemon juice
- ⅔–¾ cup (150–200 ml) neutral oil
- Salt

Sauce
- ⅔ c. (150 ml) homemade mayonnaise
- 3½ tbsp. (50 ml) sherry vinegar
- 1½ c. (350 ml) mussel broth
- Chopped chives
- Chopped tarragon
- Diced avocado
- Salt
- Black pepper
- Tabasco

Avocado Cream
- 1 c. (200 g) avocado
- 1 tbsp. + 1 tsp. (20 ml) lemon juice
- Salt

Garnish
- Diced tomato
- Avocado cream
- Cilantro microgreens

PREPARATION

Mussels

Wash the mussels thoroughly.

Dice the onion and sauté with the butter in a pot.

Add the parsley sprigs and white wine, and bring to a boil.

Immediately add the mussels, cover and cook for about 5 minutes or until they open.

Discard any that remain closed.

Transfer the mussels to a bowl.

Strain the broth and reserve.

Remove one half of each shell, leaving only the bottom shell.

Carefully detach the mussel with a knife and place it back on the bottom shell.

Repeat with each mussel.

Keep refrigerated on a tray.

Mayonnaise

In a blender, beat the egg with the mustard and salt.

Slowly add the oil in a thin stream until the mixture thickens.

When the desired thickness is reached, add the lemon juice.

Season with salt to taste.

Set aside.

Sauce

Combine the mayonnaise, vinegar, and mussel broth in a blender.

Blend until smooth.

Add the tarragon or chives if desired and continue blending.

Add some small avocado cubes for a creamier sauce.

Keep refrigerated.

Mussels Marinated with Tarragon

Avocado Cream

Blend the avocado with the lemon juice until thick and glossy.

Add salt to taste.

Set aside.

Plating

Set out small plates with a little coarse salt to arrange the mussels.

Remove each mussel from the tray, spoon a bit of sauce into the shell, and place the mussel on top.

Dot the mussel with avocado cream.

Add a few pieces of tomato to the sauce and garnish with a microgreen.

Repeat the process for each mussel.

Arrange three or four mussels on each plate and serve immediately.

Scallops with Pistachio, Soy and Balsamic Sauce

This is a very simple and delicious dish. The crunchy pistachio coating adds texture and a light sweet-salty flavor to the juicy scallops. Though not part of the original recipe, this crust allows me to introduce an extra layer of texture, as does the creaminess provided by the pea purée. It is complemented by a soy and balsamic sauce, offering a balanced mix of umami and acidity that enhances the delicacy of the scallops, creating a harmony of flavors that is both sophisticated and surprising.

4 servings

INGREDIENTS

Scallops

- 16 scallops (4 per person)
- ⅔ c. (100 g) shelled pistachios
- Clarified butter, for frying
- Balsamic vinegar
- Japanese soy sauce
- Black pepper

Pea Purée

- 1¾ c. (250 g) fresh peas
- ¾ c. + 1 tbsp. (180 ml) water
- 1 tbsp. (15 g) butter
- Salt

Garnish

- Edible flowers

PREPARATION

Pea Purée

Boil the peas in water with a pinch of salt for 5 minutes.

Immediately transfer the peas to an ice water bath to cool.

Cool the cooking water as well.

Blend the peas with a bit of the cooking water until smooth.

Strain through a fine sieve.

Season to taste and set aside.

Scallops

Finely chop the pistachios.

Dip the top of each scallop into the chopped pistachios, or alternatively, coat just the sides, leaving the top and bottom exposed.

Sear the scallops in hot clarified butter.

Remove from the pan and keep warm.

Deglaze the pan with balsamic vinegar and soy sauce.

Season with pepper.

Plating

Place a spoonful of pea purée on each plate.

Place four scallops on top of the purée.

Add a few dots of the soy-balsamic sauce.

Garnish with edible flowers.

Serve immediately.

Tiramisu Bonbon

The chef's original menu did not include dessert, but I chose to create a tiramisu variation in tribute to his role as executive chef at Roberto's, a high-end Italian restaurant. The concept: a chocolate shell filled with tiramisu, combining the crunch of bittersweet chocolate with the luscious, creamy essence of the classic Italian dessert. The tiramisu filling adds a touch of sophistication, turning this bonbon into an explosion of flavors that complement each other perfectly.

4 servings

INGREDIENTS

Tiramisu Bonbon

- 4 ladyfingers or savoiardi biscuits
- ⅔ c. (150 ml) espresso coffee
- Tiramisu cream

Tiramisu Cream

- ¾ c. + 2 tbsp. (200 g) mascarpone
- ¾ c. + 1 tbsp. (200 ml) heavy cream
- 4 egg yolks (80 g)
- ⅓ c. + 1 tbsp. (90 g) sugar
- 2 tbsp. (30 ml) water
- 1 sheet (5 g) gelatin
- 1½ tbsp. (25 ml) water (for dissolving gelatin)
- ½ tsp. vanilla extract

Cocoa *Tuile*

- 7 tbsp. (100 g) butter
- ½ c. (100 g) sugar
- 3 egg whites (100 g)
- ⅔ c. (80 g) all-purpose flour
- 3 tbsp. (20 g) unsweetened cocoa powder

Chocolate Shell

- 7 oz. (200 g) couverture chocolate

Chocolate Ganache

- ½ c. (120 ml) heavy cream
- 4¼ oz. (120 g) dark chocolate

PREPARATION

Tiramisu Cream

Combine sugar and water in a saucepan and cook until it reaches 120 °C (250 °F) to form a syrup.
While heating, beat yolks until light and fluffy.
Slowly add the hot syrup while beating continuously, until the mixture pales and doubles in volume.
Soak gelatin sheet in the water and microwave briefly to melt.
Stir the melted gelatin into the egg yolk mixture.
Soften the mascarpone and blend with the egg base.
In a separate bowl, whip the cream with the vanilla until it forms stiff peaks.
Gently fold the whipped cream into the mascarpone mix.
Transfer the mixture to a piping bag and chill.

Chocolate Shell

Finely chop the chocolate.
Place in a bowl and melt over a double boiler.
Use a pastry brush to coat the inside of silicone half-sphere molds with the chocolate.
Repeat the coating 2 or 3 times to create a solid shell with no thin or transparent spots.
Let it set completely, then set aside.

Tiramisu Bonbon

When the chocolate shells are firm, pipe the tiramisu cream into the shell.
Trim a piece of sponge or ladyfinger to fit the mold, soak it in coffee, and place it in the cream.
Wipe away any excess and freeze for a minimum of 4 hours, until the filling is frozen.

Cocoa *Tuile*

Preheat the oven to 350 °F (175 °C).
Gently melt the butter.
Combine the flour, sugar, cocoa powder, and egg whites.
Add the melted butter.
Mix until smooth.
Spread a thin layer of the batter into a silicone *tuile* mold.

Tiramisu Bonbon

Smooth with a spatula, removing any excess.
Bake for 4–6 minutes or until golden and easily released from the mold.
Remove carefully to avoid breakage and cool completely.

Chocolate Ganache
Finely chop the chocolate.
Bring the cream to a boil.
Remove from heat and add the chopped chocolate.
Stir until fully melted and glossy.
Transfer the mixture to a piping bag and set aside.

Plating
Take the tiramisu bonbons out of the freezer and carefully unmold while frozen.
Arrange on the serving dish and let sit a few minutes to soften slightly.
Pipe a few dots of tiramisu cream and chocolate ganache around the plate.
Garnish each bonbon with a *tuile* and serve immediately.

m3

- Crispy Prawn, Zucchini Carpaccio, Wasabi Mayo
- Roasted Lamb, Saffron Risotto, Rice Paper Crisps
- Caramelized Pineapple, Orange Gel and *Gelée*, Coconut Ice Cream

Chef Franz Conde

Venezuelan chef Franz Conde boasts a long-standing culinary career, both in his native country and throughout Europe, where he earned recognition as one of its leading chefs. He is currently the Executive Chef at the Hilton in Amsterdam, where he resides. His career includes roles at the Çırağan Palace Kempinski in Istanbul—then regarded as Turkey's finest hotel—Roberto's in the Netherlands, and his own restaurant, Aragua, in England. In addition, he was Executive Chef at the Athenee Palace Hilton in Bucharest and interned at top Italian restaurants such as Aimo e Nadia, Antica Osteria del Ponte, Enoteca Pinchiorri, and San Domenico.

Crispy Prawn, Zucchini Carpaccio, Wasabi Mayo

This is my own take on the original recipe, from which I kept only the main ingredient and created something more aligned with my style—something I personally love. The prawn remains crisp on the outside and tender within, paired with a zucchini carpaccio that brings freshness and acidity, perfectly balancing the dish. A final touch of wasabi mayonnaise adds a creamy, gently spicy accent.

4 servings

INGREDIENTS

Prawns
· 12 large prawns
· 1 egg
· Panko breadcrumbs
· Salt
· Black pepper

Zucchini Carpaccio
· 4 medium zucchini
· Lemon juice
· Salt

Wasabi Mayo
· 7 tbsp. (100 g) mayonnaise
· 2 tbsp. (30 g) wasabi paste

Tuile
· ⅓ c. + 1 tbsp. (50 g) all-purpose flour
· 3½ tbsp. (50 g) unsalted butter
· 2 egg whites (50 g)
· ⅛ tsp. (0.5 g) salt

Garnish
· Microgreens
· Edible flowers

PREPARATION

Prawns
Clean and peel the prawns.
Insert a wooden skewer through each prawn to keep it straight while cooking.
Beat the egg with a little salt and pepper.
Dredge the prawns in the egg, then in panko breadcrumbs until fully coated.
Set aside.

Zucchini Carpaccio
Using a mandoline, slice the zucchini lengthwise (about ⅛ inch / 2 mm thick).
Lay the slices for each serving out on a plate, slightly overlapping each slice.
Trim with a ring mold or desired shape, removing the outer edges.
Wipe the plate.
Drizzle with salt and lemon juice and set aside.
Set aside.

Wasabi Mayo
Combine mayonnaise and wasabi paste in a bowl until well blended.
Add wasabi to taste.
Transfer to a small squeeze bottle or piping bag.
Keep chilled until serving.

Tuile
Gently melt the butter.
Combine all ingredients, then spread the mixture over a mold in the desired shape.
Bake at 320 °F (160 °C) for 10 minutes.
Gently unmold to avoid breakage.

Plating
Deep-fry the prawns in hot oil.
Arrange three prawns on top of the zucchini carpaccio and add a few drops of wasabi mayo.
Finish with microgreens, edible flowers, and a *tuile* garnish.

Roasted Lamb, Saffron Risotto, Rice Paper Crisps

I made subtle changes to the original recipe to guarantee it works flawlessly, combining tradition with a modern touch. The lamb delivers succulent, tender meat full of layered, aromatic flavors. The saffron risotto pairs perfectly, offering a creamy texture, a delicate, complex flavor, and a touch of color. The rice crisp serves as a surprising element of texture and a refined decorative touch.

4-6 servings

INGREDIENTS

Lamb

- 1 leg of lamb
- 4 c. (600 g) carrot
- 1½ c. (200 g) onion
- 2 c. (400 g) tomato
- 1¾ oz. (50 g) fresh thyme
- 1 whole head of garlic
- ⅔ c. (150 g) butter
- ⅔ c. (150 ml) olive oil
- Salt
- Black pepper

Saffron Risotto

- 1¼ c. (250 g) Carnaroli or Arborio rice
- 1¼ c. (180 g) onion
- 1 c. + 2 tbsp. (250 g) butter
- ⅓ c. + 1 tbsp. (100 ml) white wine
- 6¼ c. (1.5 l) beef stock
- 1 pinch saffron
- 3½ oz. (100 g) Parmesan cheese

Rice Paper Crisps

- Rice paper
- Oil
- Microgreens and edible flowers for garnish

PREPARATION

Lamb

Chop the onions and tomatoes, and slice the carrots into rounds.
Sauté in olive oil.
Remove from heat and season with salt, pepper, and thyme sprigs.
Season the lamb generously with salt and pepper and coat it in butter.
Arrange the sautéed vegetables in a roasting pan, alternating with halved garlic cloves.
Place the lamb on top of the vegetables and cover with foil.
Roast at a low temperature, 280–300 °F (140–150 °C), for 2–3 hours until tender and juicy.
Add water during cooking if needed to keep the vegetables moist.
After 2 hours, insert a knife to test the tenderness—the timing will vary with the size and quality of the meat.
Transfer the meat to a tray, cover, and let rest.

Sauce

Place the roasting pan on the stovetop and deglaze with a splash of water.
Add 3 tablespoons (40 g) of butter and whisk until emulsified.
Strain everything into a separate pot to extract as much liquid as possible.
Reduce the sauce until it reaches a coating consistency.
Adjust the seasoning and butter until the sauce is glossy.
Set aside.

Saffron Risotto

Gently sauté the finely diced onion over low heat for 5 minutes.
Add the rice and cook for 7–8 minutes.
Stir in the saffron during the last minute of cooking.
Deglaze with the white wine and let it evaporate completely.
Slowly ladle in hot meat broth, stirring constantly.
When the rice is done, add butter and Parmesan for extra creaminess.
Season to taste and let sit for 2 minutes before serving.

Roasted Lamb, Saffron Risotto, Rice Paper Crisps

Rice Paper Crisps
Cut rice paper sheets into medium-sized triangles.
Heat neutral oil in a small saucepan.
Fry the rice paper briefly until the triangles puff up and become crisp.
Drain on paper towels and set aside.

Plating
Place a ring on a preheated plate and pack in the saffron risotto.
Carefully lift off the mold.
Add a thick slice of lamb next to the risotto.
Drizzle some sauce on top of the lamb.
Garnish the lamb with a rice paper crisp, microgreens, and edible flowers.

Caramelized Pineapple, Orange Gel and *Gelée*, Coconut Ice Cream

This dessert is light, refreshing, and delicious. While not the original recipe, I used the same ingredients in a creative new way. The caramelized pineapple, with its sweetness, acidity, and subtle smokiness, pairs beautifully with the orange gel and gelée, which enhance its citrus notes. The coconut ice cream adds creaminess and a smooth texture, giving the dish an exotic touch.

4-6 servings

INGREDIENTS

Caramelized Pineapple
· 1 whole pineapple
· 5¾ tbsp. (80 g) unsalted butter

Orange *Gelée*
· ¾ c. (175 ml) orange juice
· ¼ c. (25 g) sugar
· ½ tsp. (2 g) agar-agar

Coconut Ice Cream
· 1 c. (240 ml) coconut milk
· ½ c. (120 ml) coconut cream
· ¼ c. (60 ml) condensed milk
-or-
· 9 oz. (250 g) commercial coconut ice cream

Garnish
· Hazelnuts
· Coconut flakes
· Sugar
· Whipped cream
· Microgreens
· Edible flowers

PREPARATION

Caramelized Pineapple
Peel the pineapple and cut in lengthwise.
Cut each half into slices approximately ⅓ inch (7 mm) thick.
Using a rectangular cutter or a knife, trim each slice into 1¼ × 2½-inch (3 × 6 cm) rectangles, discarding the core and ensuring even shapes. Save the trimmings for juice or other uses. Set rectangles aside.

Orange *Gelée*
Heat the orange juice and sugar over low heat for 4 minutes.
Strain and return to heat. Stir in the agar-agar and boil for 2 minutes.
Pour into a tray and let cool until set. Cut several ¼-inch (3 mm) cubes and set aside.
Blend the remaining gel until smooth. Strain and pour into a small squeeze bottle or piping bag. Set aside.

Coconut Ice Cream
Blend the coconut milk, coconut cream and condensed milk until fully combined.
Transfer to a container and let cool.
Once cold, churn in an ice cream or sorbet maker

Garnish
Make a basic caramel. Stir in the hazelnuts and coconut flakes.
Mix with a spatula and spread onto a silicone mat to cool.
Once hardened, chop into small pieces. Whip the cream until it holds soft peaks.
Transfer to a piping bag and set aside.

Plating
Melt a small piece of butter in a non-stick pan.
Sear each pineapple slice on both sides until lightly golden.
Arrange them on the serving plate.
Add a few cubes of gelée on top of each slice.
Dot the plate with some orange gel and whipped cream.
Garnish with microgreens and edible flowers.
Place a spoonful of the nut and coconut brittle next to the pineapple and press to flatten.
Add a quenelle of coconut ice cream on top.
Serve immediately.

- Pea Cream, Truffled Quail Eggs
- Lamb *Kibbeh Nayeh*, Chickpea Cream, and Yogurt Mousse
- Marinated Salmon, Avocado Cream, Cream Cheese, and Pickle Sauce
- Pears with Gorgonzola Foam and Nut Crisp
- Lamb Croquettes, Tartar Sauce
- Dark Chocolate Cream, Olive Oil, Sea Salt Flakes, and French Toast

Chef Carlos García

A graduate of the prestigious Hofmann Culinary School in Barcelona, Spain, the Venezuelan chef Carlos García honed his craft with internships at two of the world's most acclaimed restaurants: El Bulli and El Celler de Can Roca. He is best known for bringing a bold and innovative perspective to Venezuelan cuisine at Alto, the acclaimed Caracas restaurant he founded. Building on that success, he later opened Obra in Miami, followed by a role as Executive Chef at Leku, also in Miami. His work has earned him numerous accolades, including recognition as one of Latin America's top chefs by *Latin America's 50 Best Restaurants*.

Pea Cream, Truffled Quail Eggs

This is a delicious cream soup, featuring a unique, elegant, and distinctive mix of flavors, and one of my favorites. I omitted toasted garlic and a few other ingredients from the original recipe, but its essence remains intact. The pea cream offers a sweet, subtly herbal flavor and a smooth, velvety texture, while the truffled quail egg brings an added dimension of flavor and aroma. Its rich and creamy yolk lends a luxurious silkiness, which, combined with the truffle, turns this cream soup into a true delicacy.

8-10 servings

INGREDIENTS

Pea Cream

- 4¾ c. (700 g) shelled peas
- 2¼ c. (300 g) onion
- 3 garlic cloves
- ⅓ c. + 1 tbsp. (100 ml) olive oil
- Salt

Truffled Quail Eggs

- 10 quail eggs
- Truffle oil
- Maldon salt, to taste
- Beet microgreens

PREPARATION

Pea Cream

Finely dice the onion and garlic (brunoise).
Sauté the onion and garlic in a pan with a little oil until barely translucent, without browning.
Set aside.
Bring salted water to a boil in a pot, then add the peas.
Cook until tender.
Chill immediately in an ice water bath to halt cooking and maintain their bright green color.
Cool the peas and cooking liquid completely.
Purée the cooled ingredients, adding cooking water as necessary to create a creamy consistency.
Add the sautéed onion and garlic and blend again.
Strain the mixture and set aside.

Truffled Quail Eggs

Using a paring knife, carefully crack the quail eggs.
Lay a piece of plastic wrap over a small espresso cup, pressing down slightly to form a shallow well.
Lightly brush the plastic wrap with truffle oil.
Pour the quail egg onto the plastic wrap.
Fold the plastic wrap into a small bundle and secure with kitchen twine.
Poach in boiling water for 1 minute, then immediately chill in ice water.
Set aside.

Plating

Heat the pea cream and pour it into a shot glass or short tumbler.
Cut the twine and place the quail egg on top of the pea cream.
Drizzle with olive oil, sprinkle Maldon salt, and garnish with a beet microgreen.

Lamb *Kibbeh Nayeh*, Chickpea Cream, and Yogurt Mousse

This dish is a refined fusion of textures and flavors from the Middle East. *Kibbeh Nayeh* can be prepared with either beef or lamb. Here I chose to use lamb, which delivers a soft, rich and flavorful texture when combined with the bulgur wheat and spices. The chickpea cream perfectly complements the meat's intensity, while the yogurt mousse brings balance with its delicate acidity and lightness, creating an interplay of tradition and modernity with sophisticated and harmonious flavors.

6-8 servings

INGREDIENTS

Lamb *Kibbe Nayeh*
- 14 oz. (400 g) lamb loin
- 1½ c. (200 g) No. 3 bulgur wheat
- ¼ c. (40 g) red pepper
- ¼ c. (50 g) red onion
- 2 garlic cloves
- ⅛ c. (25 g) butternut squash
- ⅛ c. (25 g) zucchini
- Za'atar, to taste
- Olive oil
- Salt
- Black pepper

Yogurt Mousse
- 2 c. (500 g) yogurt
- 1½ sheets of gelatin
- 1 c. (250 ml) heavy cream
- 1 tbsp. (15 ml) olive oil
- 2 tbsp. (30 g) fresh spearmint

Chickpea Cream
- 1 c. (200 g) cooked chickpeas
- 1 tbsp. + 1 tsp. (20 g) tahini (sesame paste)
- 1 garlic clove
- Olive oil
- Salt
- Black pepper

Garnish
- Microgreens
- Edible flowers
- Dried parsley

PREPARATION

Lamb *Kibbeh Nayeh*

Hydrate the wheat in water for 30 minutes and drain well.

Grind the frozen lamb together with the red pepper and the bulgur wheat in a food processor.

Add the remaining vegetables, cut into brunoise.

Combine everything thoroughly in a bowl set over ice to keep the mixture cold.

Season with spices, olive oil, salt, and pepper to taste.

Refrigerate.

Yogurt Mousse

Heat 3 tablespoons plus 1 teaspoon (50 ml) of the heavy cream and infuse with half of the mint leaves for 5 minutes.

Stir the pre-soaked gelatin into the warm cream until dissolved.

Whip the rest of the cream to soft peaks.

Flavor the yogurt with olive oil and the remaining chopped mint.

Combine the yogurt mixture with the gelatin cream.

Refrigerate until cold, then gently fold in the whipped cream.

Chill the yogurt mousse for at least 6 hours.

Transfer to a piping bag and set aside.

Chickpea Cream

Purée all ingredients together and season to taste.

Transfer to a piping bag and set aside.

Plating

On a chilled plate, position two differently sized rings.

Fill each ring with the *kibbeh*.

Pipe dollops of varying sizes of mousse and chickpea cream.

Garnish with microgreens, edible flowers, and parsley.

Marinated Salmon, Avocado Cream, Cream Cheese, and Pickle Sauce

In this recipe I replaced the smoked element of the original recipe with a delicate blend of cream cheese and avocado. It is a fresh, uncomplicated dish, and one that I personally love. Its elegance stems precisely from its simplicity. The marinated salmon takes on subtle, refined flavors that enhance its tender texture, while the dill adds a fragrant, aromatic note. Finally, the cheese and avocado creams, along with the acidity of the pickle sauce, complete the recipe by balancing and bringing the flavors together.

6-8 servings

INGREDIENTS

Salmon
- 14 oz. (400 g) salmon
- Fresh dill sprigs
- Olive oil
- Salt
- Black pepper

Avocado Cream
- ½ c. (120 g) avocado
- 1 tsp. (5 ml) lemon juice
- Salt, to taste

Cream Cheese Mixture
- 3½ oz. (100 g) cream cheese
- 2 tbsp. (30 ml) heavy cream
- 2 tsp. (10 ml) lemon juice
- Salt
- Black pepper

Pickle Sauce
- 2⅛ oz. (60 g) dill pickles
- 2 tsp. (10 ml) pickle brine
- ½ tsp. (1.4 g) xanthan gum

Garnish
- Dill sprigs
- Edible flowers

PREPARATION

Salmon
Dice the salmon into ¾ × ⅜-inch (2 × 1 centimeter) cubes.
Mix the salmon with a few chopped sprigs of dill.
Season with olive oil, salt, and freshly ground black pepper.

Avocado Cream
Puree the avocado until smooth and glossy.
Add the lemon juice and season with salt and pepper.
Mix well, transfer to a squeeze bottle and set aside.

Cream Cheese Mixture
Combine all ingredients until smooth.
Transfer to a piping bag and keep chilled.

Pickle Sauce
Chop the pickles and blend with the pickle brine.
Add xanthan gum and blend again until smooth.
Transfer to a squeeze bottle and set aside.

Plating
Arrange several cubes of the marinated salmon on a small plate or individual dish.
Pipe small dots of the avocado cream, cream cheese mixture and pickle sauce on top of the salmon.
Garnish with dill sprigs and edible flower petals.
Serve immediately.

Pears with Gorgonzola Foam and Nut Crisp

I completely revamped this recipe, transforming each component while keeping the flavor combination in mind. Rather than figs filled with Roquefort, I chose pears with a new preparation. I absolutely love this recipe. The pear, barely poached in a Prosecco syrup, offers a delicate sweetness. The Gorgonzola foam adds a refined touch, combining light creaminess with an intense yet delicate flavor. The nut *tuile* replaces the fig's original crust, delivering a crunchy texture and toasted nut flavors that perfectly balance the creaminess of the foam and the tenderness of the pear. A perfect blend of sweet, savory, creamy, and crunchy.

8 servings

INGREDIENTS

Pears

- 4 small pears
- ½ c. (100 g) sugar
- ⅓ c. + 1 tbsp. (100 ml) water
- ⅓ c. + 1 tbsp. (100 ml) Prosecco

Gorgonzola Foam

- 5½ oz. (150 g) Gorgonzola cheese
- 1¼ c. (300 ml) heavy cream
- Salt
- Black pepper

Nut Crisp

- 1 c. (100 g) almond flour
- ⅓ c. + 1 tbsp. (50 g) all-purpose flour
- ½ c. (100 g) granulated sugar
- ½ c. (100 g) brown sugar
- ⅓ c. + 1 tbsp. (100 ml) water
- 1 c. less 2 tbsp. (200 g) butter
- ¼–⅓ c. (30 g) chopped hazelnuts
- ¼–⅓ c. (30 g) chopped walnuts
- ¼–⅓ c. (30 g) chopped pine nuts
- ¼–⅓ c. (30 g) chopped almonds

PREPARATION

Pears

Slice the pears in half lengthwise.

Carefully scoop out the core and seeds using a parisienne scoop, creating a half-circle hollow in each pear half.

In a medium saucepan, prepare a syrup with the water, sugar, and Prosecco.

When the syrup is ready, poach the pears for 8 minutes on one side and 8 minutes on the other.

Remove the pears and place them in a serving dish.

Pour the syrup over them and set aside.

Gorgonzola Foam

Heat the heavy cream and add the Gorgonzola.

Stir until it reaches 180 °F (80 °C).

Dissolve the cheese completely and transfer the mixture to a siphon bottle.

Add two chargers and shake well. Set aside.

Nut Crisp

Toast and peel all nuts. Finely chop and set aside.

Bring water and sugar to a syrup consistency in a small saucepan.

In a bowl, combine the butter with the hot syrup.

Add the flours and stir until fully blended.

Spoon small, well-spaced circles onto a silicone baking mat.

Sprinkle each circle with the chopped nuts.

Bake at 350 °F (175 °C) for 8 minutes.

Remove from oven and let cool. Set aside

Plating

Arrange half a pear on a plate, with the flat side facing up.

Fill the hollow of each pear half with the Gorgonzola foam.

Garnish with flower petals and microgreens.

Top the foam with a nut crisp.

Serve immediately.

Lamb Croquettes, Tartar Sauce

This is one of those versatile recipes you can make with almost any protein—meat, chicken, or fish. The original recipe used ostrich, but I wanted to highlight a technique suited to trimmings of meat that benefit from slow cooking. In this version, I used sous vide lamb ossobuco trimmings. You can also use slow roasted lamb trimmings; the important thing is that the meat is tender and juicy. The finished croquette is crisp and golden outside, and meltingly tender inside. I pair them with my own take on tartar sauce, for a result that is light, fresh, and delicious. Although many associate this condiment with seafood, this adaptation works beautifully with meat as well.

6-8 servings

INGREDIENTS

Lamb

- 14 oz. (400 g) lamb shank (ossobuco)

Lamb Croquettes

- 7 oz. (200 g) lamb meat
- 1 c. + 1 tbsp. (130 g) all-purpose flour
- ½ c. (110 g) butter
- 3¾ c. (900 ml) lamb jus or beef stock
- 3 eggs (140 g)
- Flour
- Breadcrumbs
- Salt
- Whole peppercorns

Tartar Sauce

- ¾ c. + 2 tbsp. (200 g) mayonnaise
- 2 tsp. (10 g) Dijon mustard
- 2 tsp. (10 ml) lemon juice
- 3 tbsp. (50 g) pickled gherkins
- 1 tbsp. + 1 tsp. (20 g) capers
- 1 tbsp. + 1 tsp. (20 g) onion

Garnish

- Microgreens
- Edible flowers

PREPARATION

Lamb

Place the lamb shank in a vacuum-seal bag. Add salt, whole peppercorns, and olive oil.
Cook sous-vide at 160 °F (70 °C) for 24 hours. Transfer to an ice bath to cool and set aside.
Alternatively, you can roast it in the oven at 300 °F (150 °C) for 8 hours, or use leftover braised lamb.
Cut the meat into small pieces and shred it. Place in a bowl and set aside.
Save the cooking liquid for later use.

Lamb Croquettes

Make a roux by combining the butter and flour over low heat.
Set aside ½ cup (100 ml) of the lamb jus.
Heat the remaining jus or stock and slowly add it to the roux.
Let it simmer until it thickens into a silky, creamy *velouté*.
Add the shredded lamb and the remaining cooking jus.
Continue cooking until the mixture reaches a firmer consistency.
Season to taste with salt and black pepper. Transfer to a tray and cover tightly with plastic wrap.
Chill for 12 hours to firm up the mixture. Scoop and shape into 1-ounce (25 g) balls.
Dredge each ball lightly in flour, then dip in beaten egg, and finally coat with breadcrumbs.
Set aside.

Tartar Sauce

Finely dice the pickled gherkins, capers, and onion.
Combine all the ingredients with the mayonnaise and Dijon mustard and keep chilled.

Plating

Fry the lamb croquettes in oil at 375 °F (190 °C) just before serving.
Remove the croquettes from the pan and blot excess oil with paper towels.
Arrange the lamb croquettes on a serving plate.
Serve with tartar sauce in a small dish, or add small dollops directly on the plate.
Garnish with a microgreen and edible flowers, and serve immediately.

Dark Chocolate Cream, Olive Oil, Sea Salt Flakes, and French Toast

This dessert is spectacular: a sophisticated creation with a unique balance of sweet and savory. The velvety texture and bold flavor of the dark chocolate cream envelop the palate with deep intensity. The olive oil enhances the richness of the chocolate, adding an unexpected note, and the salt flakes—delicate but essential—elevate the entire flavor profile. The French toast rounds out the dish perfectly, balancing the intensity of the chocolate with a warm, crisp, and airy element.

6-8 servings

INGREDIENTS

Dark Chocolate Cream

- 7 oz. (200 g) 70% dark chocolate
- 1 c. (250 ml) heavy cream
- 1 c. (250 ml) milk
- ⅓ c. (75 g) sugar
- 5 egg yolks

French Toast

- Brioche
- 1 c. (250 ml) milk
- ⅓ c. (75 g) sugar
- 3 eggs

Garnish

- 7 oz. (200 g) couverture chocolate
- Olive oil
- Maldon salt
- Edible flower (optional)

PREPARATION

Dark Chocolate Cream

Make a *crème anglaise.*
Bring the milk and cream to a boil.
Whisk the egg yolks together with the sugar until pale.
Slowly add the hot milk and cream to the yolk mixture while whisking continuously.
Strain this mixture through a sieve and return to heat until it reaches 175 °F (80 °C).
Dissolve the chopped chocolate in the hot mixture.
Transfer to a rectangular dish and chill in the refrigerator for at least 12 hours.

Garnish

Melt the chocolate and spread a layer approximately ½ inch (2 mm) thick onto an acetate sheet.
Allow to cool and cut into 1¼ × 2-inch (3 × 5 cm) rectangles.
Use ⅜-inch and ¾-inch round cutters (1 and 2 cm) to punch out holes of different sizes, revealing the surface below.
Set aside.
In a separate step, fill a piping bag with a little of the melted chocolate.

French Toast

Slice the brioche into ½-inch (1.5 cm) slices.
Trim each slice into rectangles approximately 1¼ × 2 inches (3 × 5 cm).
Whisk the eggs with the sugar until pale, then add the milk.
Soak each brioche rectangle in the *crème anglaise*, coating both sides.
Brown in a nonstick pan with butter until golden on both sides.

Plating

On a plate, draw two intersecting lines with the melted chocolate.
Place the toasted brioche slice to one side of the plate.
Pipe dots of the dark chocolate cream on top.
Drizzle a few drops of olive oil and sprinkle with Maldon salt flakes.
Lay the chocolate garnish over the cream and serve immediately.

m5

- Pita Crisp, Goat Cheese Cream, Blackberry Caviar
- Mussel Trio in the Shell, Tomato Soup
- Airy *Cachapa*, *Queso de Mano* Mousse, Corn *Tuile*
- Chicken Lollipops, Honey Mustard
- Upside-Down Meringue Kisses, Strawberry and Blackberry

Chef John Guerrero

With several decades of culinary experience under his belt, John Guerrero began his career in the kitchens of the Café Olé restaurant chain in Caracas in the late 1990s. His drive to continue learning eventually took him to Spain, where he worked in various restaurants across the Canary Islands and Madrid. For some time now, Guerrero has been focused on culinary consulting through his own company, Chefbusiness. Beyond the kitchen, he is passionate about new technologies and their application both within and beyond the realm of gastronomy.

Pita Crisp, Goat Cheese Cream, Blackberry Caviar

This starter is simple yet combines contrasting textures and complex flavors, offering a unique sensory experience. The pita crisp serves as the perfect base for a creamy goat cheese with a subtly tangy and earthy flavor that contrasts delightfully with the fruity notes of the blackberry caviar. These small, glossy spheres gently burst in the mouth, adding an attractive and unexpected element to the dish, showcasing a modern and playful culinary technique.

6 servings

INGREDIENTS

Blackberry Caviar

- ⅓ c. + 1 tbsp. (100 g) blackberry purée
- 2 tsp. (10 ml) liquid glucose
- 2 tsp. (10 g) sugar
- ¼ tsp. (1 g) agar-agar
- 1¾ c. (400 ml) sunflower oil

Goat Cream Cheese

- 6⅓ oz. (180 g) goat cheese
- 4 tbsp. (60 ml) heavy cream
- Salt
- Black pepper

Pita Crisp

- 2 pita bread rounds
- Olive oil

Garnish

- Microgreens

PREPARATION

Blackberry Caviar

Mix all ingredients, except the oil, in a blender until smooth and velvety.

Strain the mixture.

Pour the sunflower oil into a bowl and place in an ice bath.

Cool the oil to between 60 and 63 °F (15–17 °C).

Alternatively, chill the oil in the freezer for 20–30 minutes.

Keep the blackberry and agar-agar solution at about 175 °F (80 °C) to maintain it in liquid form.

Fill a syringe with half the blackberry solution and half air to allow movement.

Shake the syringe and drop hundreds of small droplets into the tempered oil, which will form the blackberry caviar when strained.

Set aside.

Goat Cream Cheese

Blend all the ingredients in a bowl.

Transfer to a piping bag and set aside.

Pita Crisp

Cut the pita bread into triangles and split it in half for thinner crisps.

Arrange on a baking sheet and drizzle with olive oil.

Bake at 250 °F (120 °C) for 1 hour or until golden and crisp.

Remove from the oven and let cool.

Set aside.

Plating

Place 3 pieces of crispy pita on a plate.

Pipe several dots of goat cheese cream onto the pita.

Add a teaspoon of blackberry caviar next to each dot of cheese cream.

Garnish with microgreens and serve.

Mussel Trio in the Shell, Tomato Soup

Only the mussels were part of the original recipe. For this version, I chose to present them differently, paired with a tomato sauce. Personally, this is how I enjoy them most, because it is a taste of the sea with a Mediterranean touch. The mussels are prepared in the traditional way but are served in their shell with a light, vibrant tomato sauce that complements them perfectly with its natural acidity and subtle sweetness.

4 servings

INGREDIENTS

Mussel Trio
- 12 large fresh mussels
- ⅔ c. (100 g) onion
- 3½ tbsp. (50 ml) white wine
- Coarse salt

Tomato Sauce
- 1 c. (250 g) canned peeled tomato
- ⅔ c. (100 g) onion
- 5 garlic cloves
- 2½ tsp. (15 g) salt
- 2 tsp. (10 g) sugar
- Fresh basil

Garnish
- Basil microgreens
- Edible flower petals

PREPARATION

Mussel Trio

Wash the mussels thoroughly and set aside.

Dice the onion and sauté in a pot with a little olive oil.

Add the white wine and bring to a boil.

Immediately add the mussels to the pot, cover and cook for about 5 minutes or until they open.

Discard any that remain closed.

Remove the top shell and carefully loosen the mussel with a knife.

Set the mussels aside with the bottom shells.

Tomato Sauce

Purée the onion and garlic.

In a pot, sauté the puréed onion and garlic in plenty of olive oil until golden.

Add the tomato and bring to a boil.

When it begins to boil, add the basil, salt, and sugar.

Simmer over low heat for 30 minutes or until reduced by one third.

Remove the basil leaves and blend the sauce using an immersion blender.

Adjust salt to taste.

Keep warm and set aside.

Plating

Spoon a bit of coarse salt onto a small plate to form a base for three mussels.

Spoon hot tomato sauce into each mussel shell.

Set the mussel on top of the sauce, then arrange the shells on the coarse salt so that they remain stable.

Garnish with microgreens and edible flower petals.

Serve immediately.

Airy *Cachapa, Queso de Mano* Mousse, Corn *Tuile*

This plate offers a unique and inventive interplay of Venezuelan textures and flavors. The cachapa is light and fluffy, bringing a subtle corn sweetness to the palate. It is accompanied by a smooth *queso de mano* mousse, its delicate hint of saltiness provides the perfect counterpoint to the corn's natural sweetness. To complete the experience, the cachapa *tuile* adds a crunchy dimension and sophistication—a refined nod to the classic *cachapa*.

6 servings

INGREDIENTS

Airy *Cachapa*

- 3 c. (400 g) fresh corn kernels
- ⅓ c. (40 g) all-purpose flour
- 3 tbsp. + 1 tsp. (40 g) sugar
- ½ c. (100 ml) milk
- 1½ tsp. (8 g) salt
- 2 tsp. (10 ml) oil

***Queso de Mano* Mousse**

- 7 oz. (200 g) *queso de mano*
- ⅓ c. + 1 tbsp. (100 ml) heavy cream
- ⅓ c. + 1 tbsp. (100 ml) milk
- Salt

Corn *Tuile*

- ⅓ c. + 1 tbsp. (100 ml) cachapa batter

Garnish

- Edible flowers
- Microgreens

PREPARATION

Cachapa

In a blender, combine the corn, milk, sugar, and salt.
Add the flour and oil. Blend again until you achieve a thick but smooth batter.
Lightly oil a nonstick frying pan.
Pour a tablespoon of the batter into the pan, spreading it like a crepe.
Cook over medium heat on both sides until golden brown.
Repeat with the remaining batter, keeping the *cachapas* covered to stay warm.

***Queso de Mano* Mousse**

Heat the cream and the milk in a small saucepan over medium heat.
Add the finely chopped *queso de mano* and stir until melted.
Remove from heat and blend at high speed.
Transfer the mixture to a siphon bottle and chill for a minimum of 12 hours.

Corn *Tuile*

Spoon some of the cachapa batter into a *tuile* mold.
Use a spatula to evenly spread the mixture.
Fill the mold completely and wipe away any excess.
Bake at 300 °F (150 °C) for 5–7 minutes or until golden.
Remove from the oven and carefully lift while hot to avoid breakage.
Let cool and set aside.

Plating

Use a 2-inch (5-cm) ring or the shape of your choice to cut the *cachapas*.
Arrange the *cachapa* on the serving plate.
Insert two cartridges into the siphon bottle and shake vigorously.
Pipe the mousse onto the *cachapa*.
Top the foam with a corn *tuile*.
Garnish with edible flowers and serve immediately.

Chicken Lollipops, Honey Mustard

These chicken lollipops were not part of the original menu, but I find this preparation both delicious and fun. The chicken is shaped into small lollipops, with a crispy outer layer and juicy, tender meat inside—an ideal way to enjoy chicken wings. The honey mustard sauce adds a sweet and slightly tangy note that complements the chicken beautifully, balancing juiciness and crunch, sweetness and heat.

6-8 servings

INGREDIENTS

Chicken Lollipops

- About 10½ oz. (300 g, or 18 to 24) chicken wings
- Flour
- Egg
- Breadcrumbs
- Salt and whole peppercorns

Honey Mustard

- ⅔ c. (150 g) mayonnaise
- 1½ tbsp. (30 g) mustard
- 2 tbsp. (30 ml) honey

Garnish

- Microgreens
- Edible flowers

PREPARATION

Chicken Lollipops

Cut the chicken wings into two parts (drumette and wingette).

Use the drumette, and leave the wingette and tip for another recipe.

Beginning at the thin end, use a paring knife to scrape the meat from the bone halfway up the drumette.

Grasp the exposed bone with one hand, and with the other, pull the meat up until the skin is on the inside, leaving a small ball of chicken on the fat end.

Repeat with each drumette.

Season with salt and pepper.

Bread each lollipop in the traditional way: first flour, then egg, and finally breadcrumbs.

Set aside.

Honey Mustard

Combine all ingredients until smooth.

Adjust salt and sweetness to taste.

Keep chilled until serving.

Plating

Fry the chicken lollipops in hot oil just before serving.

Blot off any excess oil with a paper towel.

Brush the plate with a swipe of honey mustard and add a few extra dots of sauce.

Arrange 3 chicken lollipops bone-side up in the center of the plate.

Garnish with microgreens and edible flowers.

Serve immediately.

Upside-Down Meringue Kisses, *Dulce de Leche*, Strawberry and Blackberry

Although this dessert was not part of the original menu, I wanted to create a modern take on a traditional sweet, offering a delightful combination of light textures and fresh flavors. The crisp meringue is airy and delicate, serving as a perfect base for the *dulce de leche* with its caramelized flavor, creating a balance between lightness and indulgence. The strawberries and blackberries provide a refreshing contrast, their natural acidity cutting through the sweetness of the meringue and *dulce de leche*, crowned with a cloud of whipped cream. Finally, the strawberry gel enhances the fruity notes and lends an elegant, contemporary aesthetic to the dish.

4-6 servings

INGREDIENTS

Meringue Kisses
- 4 egg whites (125 g)
- 1¼ c. (250 g) sugar

Dulce de Leche
- 2 c. (500 ml) heavy cream
- ¾ c. (150 g) sugar
- Pinch of salt

Whipped Cream
- 1 c. (250 ml) heavy cream
- ¼ c. (50 g) sugar

Strawberry Gel
- ⅔ c. (170 ml) strawberry juice
- 2 tbsp. + 2 tsp. (30 g) sugar
- ½ tsp. (2 g) agar-agar

Garnish
- 1 c. (150 g) strawberries
- 1 c. (150 g) blackberries
- Fresh mint leaves

PREPARATION

Meringue Kisses

Combine the egg whites and sugar in a bowl.

Cook over a double boiler, stirring continuously until the sugar dissolves.

Transfer the mixture to the bowl of an electric mixer and beat at high speed until stiff peaks form.

Fill a piping bag with a plain tip.

Pipe small dots of meringue onto a baking sheet lined with a silicone mat or parchment paper.

For a different presentation, pipe 2 lines of 3 meringues each, touching lightly along their length.

Bake at 185 °F (85 °C) for approximately 2 hours.

Remove from oven and set aside.

Dulce de Leche

Place the sugar in a pan and cook over medium-high heat.

When the sugar starts to melt and caramelize to a dark amber color, stir with a wooden spoon (never metal) until all the sugar is caramelized and fully liquid.

Add the heavy cream, reserving 2 tablespoons (30 ml).

Continue stirring, though the mixture may solidify at first.

Remove from heat once the mixture is as smooth as possible; some lumps may remain.

Add the remaining heavy cream and blend with a mixer.

Reheat and add a pinch of salt, stirring until the mixture reduces slightly and achieves a smooth, creamy texture.

Transfer to a bowl and cover with plastic wrap.

Chill for at least 4 hours.

Remove when cold and transfer some *dulce de leche* to a piping bag.

Set aside.

Whipped Cream

Beat the heavy cream with sugar until stiff peaks form.

Transfer to a piping bag fitted with a star tip.

Set aside.

Upside-Down Meringue Kisses, *Dulce de Leche*, Strawberry and Blackberry

Strawberry Gel

Heat the strawberry juice and the sugar.

Add the agar-agar and bring to a boil, stirring constantly.

Remove from heat and pour into a tray.

Cover with plastic wrap pressed against the surface to prevent a film from forming on top.

Chill until firm, about 2 hours.

Remove from tray and blend until smooth and glossy.

Pour into a small squeeze bottle or piping bag.

Set aside.

Plating

Turn over the two rows of meringues onto a plate so that they rest on their peaks, with the flat side facing up.

Add dots of *dulce de leche* to each meringue.

Pipe dots of whipped cream on top of each *dulce de leche* dot, large enough so they stick together.

Arrange 1⁄16-inch (2 mm) slices of strawberries alternating with blackberries.

Garnish with small mint leaves.

Draw a dotted line with the strawberry gel and serve immediately.

m6

· *Pasta e Fagioli, Tradizionale e Moderna*

· *Tagliatelle* with Lobster "Al Graspo de Ua"

· *Fagottini di Manzo*, Montepulciano Sauce

· Orange Cannoli in Two Versions:
Crisp Cannolo, Chocolate Cannolo

Chef Carlo Lazzaron

The Italian chef Carlos Lazzaron was widely recognized as an ambassador of Venetian cuisine on the international stage. His legacy was cemented at the renowned Antico Pignolo restaurant, near Piazza San Marco in Venice, where he led the kitchen. A chef of eclectic tastes and boundless creativity, he also distinguished himself at several other acclaimed restaurants, including Taverna La Fenice, Canova at the Luna Hotel Baglioni, Harry's Bar in Venice, and Al Graspo de Ua. Tragically, Lazzaron—an avid motorcycle enthusiast—died in a fatal accident in 2015.

Pasta e Fagioli, Tradizionale e Moderna

Pasta e fagioli is a traditional dish of Italian cuisine. This rustic soup combines beans and pasta in a savory, aromatic base for a nourishing and flavorful culinary experience. The beans most commonly used are Cannellini or borlotti, lending creaminess and a mild flavor. The pasta is usually small, such as ditalini or macaroni, which blends smoothly into the soup. Once a modest peasant dish, *pasta e fagioli* has made its way onto refined restaurant menus. My version is a more elegant reinterpretation that reimagines the use of every ingredient. The dense and velvety broth remains faithful to tradition, the ravioli are delicate parcels filled with a creamy *fagioli* puree that captures the essence of the stew, and the *minestra* serves as a unifying thread.

4 servings

INGREDIENTS

Pasta e Fagioli Tradizionale

- 14 oz. (400 g) ditalini or macaroni
- 7 oz. (200 g) dried cannellini or white beans
- 2 c. (500 g) canned peeled tomato
- 1 c. (100 g) celery stalks
- 2¾ oz. (80 g) pancetta
- 3½ tbsp. (50 ml) extra virgin olive oil
- 1 garlic clove
- Parmigiano Reggiano
- Fresh basil
- Salt
- Black pepper

Pasta e Fagioli Moderna

- 1 c. (250 g) reserved *pasta e fagioli tradizionale* (without the pasta, as explained in the preparation section)
- 40 wonton wrappers

Garnish

- Micro basil leaves
- Micro arugula
- Edible flower petals

PREPARATION

Pasta e Fagioli Tradizionale

Rinse the beans and place them in a large pot with about 3 quarts (3 l) of cold water.

Cover the pot and bring to a boil.

Add the finely chopped celery and garlic, one tablespoon of salt, and a few basil leaves.

Add the diced canned tomatoes.

Cook the beans for 2 hours, stirring occasionally and checking often.

Add the chopped pancetta, olive oil, and adjust the salt.

Continue cooking for about another hour, until the beans are soft but not falling apart.

Set aside 1 cup (250 g) of the *minestra* to use in the modern version preparation.

Add the pasta and cook until al dente.

Taste and adjust seasoning as needed.

Set aside.

Pasta e Fagioli Moderna

Drain the reserved *pasta e fagioli tradizionale* (without pasta) using a large strainer.

Save the broth in a pot to reheat later.

Blend the solids until you obtain a thick, creamy mixture.

Take two wonton wrappers and place a spoonful of the *fagioli* mixture in the center of one of the wrappers.

Moisten the edges with water and place the second wrapper on top. Press gently to seal.

Using a cutter, trim into circles of different sizes as you go.

Cook in salted water with a dash of oil to aid handling.

Remove immediately and place on a lightly oiled tray.

Set aside.

Pasta e Fagioli, Tradizionale e Moderna

Plating

Pasta e Fagioli Tradizionale

Reheat the *minestra*.
Ladle into warmed shallow bowls.
Add a delicate drizzle of olive oil and season with freshly ground pepper.
Garnish with micro basil leaves.
Accompany with grated Parmesan cheese.

Pasta e Fagioli Moderna

Heat the reserved broth.
Let it reduce slightly to concentrate the flavor.
Arrange 6 or 7 *fagioli* ravioli of varying sizes on a preheated plate.
Spoon over a bit of the broth.
Add a few drops of olive oil and season with freshly ground pepper.
Place some thin slices of Parmesan on top of the ravioli.
Garnish with micro arugula and edible flower petals.
Serve immediately.

Tagliatelle with Lobster "Al Graspo de Ua"

This is a perfect dish for all pasta enthusiasts. Here, I have simplified the ingredients a bit to highlight the lobster, but the technique and flavors remain unique. It combines the delicacy of *tagliatelle* with the intensity of seafood and the creaminess of a sauce made from fresh ingredients. The perfectly cooked lobster offers a juicy, tender texture, resulting in a refined pasta with a very delicate flavor. The distinctive touch from Al Graspo de Ua, which recalls Venetian tradition, is noticeable in its subtle wine note; here, a white wine that brings balance and freshness.

4 servings

INGREDIENTS

Pasta with Lobster

- 2 medium lobsters, about 18 oz. (500 g) each
- 14 oz. (400 g) fresh *tagliatelle*
- 2⅔ c. (600 ml) *passata* (strained tomato purée)
- ⅓ c. + 1 tbsp. (100 ml) dry white wine
- 2 garlic cloves
- *Peperoncino* (red chili flakes)
- 1½ tbsp. (20 g) butter
- Extra virgin olive oil
- Salt
- Black pepper

Tomato Sauce

- ⅔ c. (100 g) onion
- ⅔ c. (100 g) carrot
- ⅔ c. (100 g) celery
- 2 garlic cloves
- 14-oz. (400 g) can San Marzano peeled tomatoes
- Extra virgin olive oil

Garnish

- Microgreens or chopped parsley

PREPARATION

Tomato Sauce

Finely dice the onion, carrots and celery.

Heat enough olive oil in a medium saucepan to cover the bottom.

Add the onion and sauté for a few minutes until translucent.

Add the garlic and celery, stirring carefully to prevent the garlic from browning.

Add the carrot and sauté for 4 minutes.

Turn the heat up slightly, then add the chopped peeled tomatoes and their juice.

Simmer for 30 minutes, stirring often.

Purée until smooth.

Set aside.

Lobster Sauce

Separate the lobster tails from the heads.

Cook the tails in boiling water for 1 to 2 minutes, just enough to loosen the meat from the shell.

Remove from boiling water and transfer to a bowl of ice water.

Do the same with the claws and extract the lobster meat.

Split the underside of the tail shell and carefully remove the meat.

Slice the lobster tail meat.

In a large pot, sauté the garlic and *peperoncino* in olive oil.

Sauté the lobster meat briefly in this oil, without fully cooking it; remove and set aside.

Add the lobster shells and heads, and brown for a few minutes in the same oil.

Add the wine and reduce until the alcohol has almost evaporated.

Add the *passata* and a knob of butter.

Adjust salt and pepper to taste.

Cook for about 20 minutes.

Strain the sauce and set aside.

Tagliatelle with Lobster "Al Graspo de Ua"

Pasta with Lobster

Heat the lobster sauce and add the tomato sauce.
Cook for a few minutes, stirring until well blended.
Adjust salt and *peperoncino* to taste.
Add the lobster tail meat and any extracted claw meat.
Cook the pasta separately until al dente.
Once cooked, drain and reserve some of the cooking water.
Add the pasta to the sauce and toss to coat.
Add reserved water if needed to ensure the pasta is well coated without making the sauce too thick.

Plating

Serve the pasta in a warmed shallow bowl, with pieces of lobster on top.
Garnish with microgreens or finely chopped parsley and a drizzle of extra virgin olive oil.

Fagottini di Manzo, Montepulciano Sauce

Fagottini di manzo in Montepulciano sauce is a traditional Italian dish featuring small stuffed beef rolls cooked in red wine sauce. This recipe highlights Italy's culinary tradition of using local, seasonal ingredients to create bold, satisfying dishes. The use of Montepulciano wine not only enhances the flavor and adds depth to the sauce, but also emphasizes the importance of regional wines in Italian gastronomy.

4 servings

INGREDIENTS

Fagottini di Manzo
- 4 beef tenderloin paillards
- 4¼ oz. (120 g) mozzarella cheese
- ⅓ c. + 1 tbsp. (100 ml) Montepulciano d'Abruzzo wine
- Flour
- Salt
- Black pepper
- Oil

Potatoes
- 4 potatoes
- Butter

Garnish
- Chives
- Microgreens
- Edible flower petals

PREPARATION

Fagottini di Manzo

Lay out the beef paillard and dredge in all-purpose flour.

Cut the mozzarella into rectangles measuring about 4 to 4¾ inches (10–12 cm) long and ½ inch (1 cm) wide.

Wrap each mozzarella stick in a beef paillard. with a wooden skewer or toothpick.

Brown the rolls in a frying pan.

Remove the meat and deglaze the pan with Montepulciano wine.

Allow the sauce to reduce.

Set aside.

Potatoes

Add the peeled potatoes to a pot of salted water.

Bring to a boil, and then remove from heat.

Slice the potatoes into rounds ½ inch (1 cm) thick.

Use a 1¼-inch (3 cm) round cutter to punch out circles in the potato.

Pan-fry the potato rounds in butter until golden.

Set aside.

Plating

Spoon a tablespoon of hot wine sauce onto a warmed plate.

Arrange one *fagottino di manzo* on top, accompanied by a few potato rounds.

Garnish the *fagottino* with finely chopped chives.

Garnish the potatoes with microgreens and edible petals.

Serve immediately.

Orange Cannoli in Two Versions: Crisp Cannolo, Chocolate Cannolo

This dessert is my reinterpretation of the classic Sicilian cannoli, with contrasts in textures and flavors. The first cannolo closely resembles the traditional version, with a golden, crisp shell filled with lightly sweetened, orange-infused ricotta cream. The fine candied orange threads add slightly bitter, citrusy notes, balancing the creaminess of the ricotta. The second cannolo is chocolate, with a crisp texture, and a firm yet velvety bite. The ricotta filling enhances the aromas and intensifies the depth of the chocolate, achieving the perfect balance between tradition and reinvention.

4-6 servings

INGREDIENTS

Crisp Cannolo
- 1¼ c. (250 g) sugar
- ½ c. + 1 tbsp. (125 g) butter
- ⅓ c. + 1 tbsp. (100 ml) orange juice
- ½ c. (60 g) all-purpose flour
- 1 tbsp. (10 g) orange zest
- 1 tsp. (5 g) lemon zest

Chocolate Cannolo
- 9 oz. (250 g) couverture chocolate

Candied Orange
- 2 oranges
- ¾ c. (150 g) sugar
- Water

Cannoli Filling
- 18 oz. (500 g) ricotta cheese
- ½ c. (100 g) sugar
- 2 tbsp. (20 g) candied orange
- 1 tbsp. (10 g) orange zest
- 1 tsp. (5 g) lemon zest

Garnish
- ¾ c. (100 g) pistachios
- 3½ oz. (100 g) dark chocolate
- ⅓ c. + 1 tbsp. (100 ml) heavy cream
- Edible flowers

PREPARATION

Crisp Cannolo

Melt the butter.
Combine the butter, sugar, and orange juice in a mixing bowl.
Stir in the flour, orange zest, and lemon zest.
Mix well and chill for a minimum of 3 hours.
Line a baking tray with a silicone mat.
Form 2-inch (5 cm) squares of the batter on the tray.
Bake at 350 °F (175 °C) for 4–5 minutes or until golden brown.
Remove from the oven and straighten the squares with a spatula while still soft.
Wait 1 or 2 minutes before handling the cannoli shells.
Wrap the soft dough around a cannoli mold or similar cylinder.
Allow to cool and harden in place.
Gently slide off the mold and set the cannolo aside.

Chocolate Cannolo

Finely chop the coverture chocolate.
Melt over a double boiler.
Line the inside of a cannoli mold with a sheet of acetate.
Pour the melted chocolate into the mold over a tray.
Coat the inside with a 1–2 mm thick layer, similar to a bonbon shell.
Allow to cool and harden in place.
Carefully slide out the acetate cylinder.
Peel off the acetate and refrigerate the chocolate cannolo.

Orange Cannoli in Two Versions: Crisp Cannolo, Chocolate Cannolo

Candied Orange

Wash the orange and slice off the peel in 1–2 mm thick strips, avoiding the bitter white pith.

Flatten the orange peels on a board and remove any remaining pith, which will help avoid any bitter aftertaste.

Blanch the peels 3 times, discarding and renewing the water each time.

Make a syrup with the sugar and 2 tablespoons of water.

Heat gently until the sugar fully dissolves into a clear syrup.

Add the strips of orange peel.

Reduce to low and simmer the peels in syrup for 1 hour.

Allow to cool and store the syrup with the oranges in a glass container.

Take out a few strips, drain, and cut into very fine julienne.

Then cut the julienned strips into two or three pieces, each about ¾ inch (1.5 cm) thick.

Set aside.

Cannoli Filling

Measure the ricotta into a mixing bowl.

Break it up gently with the back of a fork.

Add the sugar and mix until fully combined.

Add the orange and lemon zests.

Stir in the finely chopped candied orange.

Mix well and transfer to a piping bag.

Set aside.

Garnish

Prepare a traditional chocolate ganache.

Chop the chocolate into small bits.

Bring the cream to a boil.

Remove from heat and add the chopped chocolate.

Stir until the ganache is smooth and glossy.

Transfer to a piping bag and set aside.

Finely chop the pistachios to decorate the ends of the cannoli.

Plating

Fill both types of cannoli with the ricotta and orange mixture.

Put the chopped pistachios in a small dish.

Dip the ends of each cannolo into the pistachio so it adheres to the filling, ensuring both ends are coated.

Arrange one crisp and one chocolate cannolo side by side on a rectangular plate.

Add a few dots of ganache and garnish with edible flower petals.

Serve immediately.

m7

- Sea Bass Ceviche with Vodka *Gelée*
- Lobster Risotto with Whiskey
- Chocolate Fondant with Rum Chocolate Sauce and *Crème Anglaise*

Chef Edgar Leal

Trained at the Culinary School of New York, Venezuelan chef Edgar Leal has left a significant mark on both the national and international food scenes. He is regarded as one of Venezuela's top chefs and a pioneer of the country's gastronomic movement. His innovative and avant-garde cooking style, refined during internships with Daniel Boulud in New York and Ferran Adrià at El Bulli, led to his recognition as a James Beard Foundation Award finalist. He is also known for a string of acclaimed restaurants, including Leal in Caracas and Cacao in Coral Gables, Miami, the latter praised for its precision and artistry in the kitchen, earning accolades from Zagat and *Food & Wine*.

Sea Bass Ceviche with Vodka *Gelée*

For this recipe, I presented a refined twist on the traditional ceviche. I altered the cut to resemble a *tiradito*—slightly thicker—but still prepared as ceviche. The presentation is distinctive, evoking a deconstructed ceviche in which the freshness of the fish is complemented by the bright acidity of the marinade. Elements like the *ají*, with its gentle heat, and the onion, with its sweet note, add texture and crispness to the dish. The cilantro appears both as fresh leaves and infused oil, lending a unique herbal character. Together, they create a dish bursting with fresh, vibrant flavors.

4 servings

INGREDIENTS

Ceviche

· 14 oz. (400 g) sea bass
· ⅔ c. (150 ml) lemon juice
· 2 tbsp. (30 g) *ají limo* (Peruvian chili pepper)
· ¾ oz. (20 g) cilantro
· 2 tbsp. (20 g) red onion

Guacamole

· 1 ripe avocado
· 2 tsp. (10 ml) lemon juice
· Salt
· Black pepper

Vodka *Gelée*

· ⅓ c. + 1 tbsp. (100 ml) Smirnoff orange vodka
· ⅓ c. + 1 tbsp. (100 ml) orange juice
· 2 tbsp. (20 g) unflavored gelatin

Cilantro Oil

· 1 oz. (30 g) cilantro
· ⅔ c. (150 ml) sunflower oil
· Salt

Garnish

· Microgreens

PREPARATION

Ceviche

Thinly slice the fish.
Slice the *ají* into thin rounds.
Finely julienne the red onion.
Select the smallest cilantro leaves.
Arrange the fish slices on a tray, sprinkle with a pinch of salt, and let them rest for a few minutes.
Add enough fresh lemon juice to cover the fish completely.
Transfer to the refrigerator and chill until ready to serve.

Guacamole

Purée the avocado until smooth and velvety.
Add the lemon juice and season with salt and pepper.
Stir to combine thoroughly.
Transfer to a squeeze bottle and keep refrigerated.

Vodka *Gelée*

Bloom the gelatin in a bowl of ice water for 10 minutes.
Bring the orange juice to a boil in a small saucepan.
Stir in the gelatin until completely dissolved, then strain through a fine mesh.
Stir in the vodka gently to combine.
Transfer the liquid to a shallow dish and chill until firm.
Once fully set, dice the gelée into neat little cubes.
Keep chilled until ready to serve.

Cilantro Oil

Briefly blanch the cilantro in boiling water, then shock in ice water to preserve color and freshness.
Drain thoroughly to remove any remaining moisture.
Blend the cilantro with the sunflower oil until fully emulsified.
Strain through a fine cloth into a clean jar and let settle.
When ready to use, decant carefully into a squeeze bottle, avoiding the sediment.

Sea Bass Ceviche with Vodka Gelée

Plating

Arrange the fish slices on a plate, folding them gently to create soft ribbons.

Add a few spoonfuls of the *leche de tigre* (the marinating liquid) to moisten the fish.

Add several small dots of guacamole to each slice.

Garnish with cubes of vodka gelée.

Drizzle with cilantro oil and garnish with cilantro leaves, sliced *ají*, red onion, and microgreens.

Serve immediately.

Lobster Risotto with Whiskey

This risotto is absolutely delicious! I've pared back the original recipe, removing several ingredients and slightly altering the cooking of the lobster so it remains tender and juicy, with its sweet, delicate flavor. The subtle smokiness and oaky notes of the whisky give the dish a layered complexity, enhancing the lobster's natural flavors and imparting a unique depth to the overall composition.

4 servings

INGREDIENTS

Lobster

- 4 lobster tails
- 1 c. (250 ml) lobster bisque
- 1 c. less 2 tsp. (230 ml) heavy cream
- 2 tbsp. (30 ml) whiskey

Lobster Bisque

- Shells from 4 lobster tails
- ⅔ c. (100 g) onion
- ⅓ c. (50 g) carrot
- ⅓ c. (50 g) celery
- ¼ c. (30 g) leek
- 2 tbsp. (30 g) tomato paste
- 2 tbsp. (30 g) butter
- 2 tbsp. + 2 tsp. (40 ml) olive oil
- 2 qt. (2 l) water
- Salt

Risotto

- 2 c. (400 g) arborio rice
- ⅓ c. (50 g) onion (brunoise)
- 1¾ c. (400 ml) white wine
- 2 c. (450 ml) fish stock
- 2 c. (450 ml) lobster bisque
- ½ c. (120 g) butter

Garnish

- Microgreens
- Edible flower petals

PREPARATION

Lobster

Boil the lobster tails for 3 to 4 minutes, depending on the size.

Remove the meat from the shells, and set the shells aside.

Slice the lobster meat into rounds about ⅞ inch (2 cm) thick. Set aside.

Lobster Bisque

Finely dice the onion, carrot, celery, and leek. Set aside.

Sear the lobster shells in a pot with olive oil.

Add the chopped vegetables and sauté, stirring occasionally, for about 3 minutes.

Stir in the tomato paste and mix well. Add the cold water and season with a little salt.

When it reaches a boil, reduce the heat to a simmer. Skim off the foam as it cooks.

Simmer until the liquid is reduced by half. Strain through a fine sieve, stir in the butter, and set aside.

Lobster in Whiskey Sauce

Melt a bit of butter in a pan and gently sear the lobster slices. Remove and set aside.

Deglaze the pan with the whisky. Stir in the lobster bisque and the cream.

Add the lobster and simmer for 2 minutes. Set aside.

Risotto

Heat the fish stock in a saucepan.

Melt the butter in a separate pan, and sauté the finely diced onion until soft and translucent.

Stir in the rice and toast for 2 to 3 minutes. Deglaze with white wine and cook, stirring constantly, until nearly evaporated.

Add about 2 cups of fish stock. Stir continuously until most of the liquid is absorbed.

Continue adding the lobster bisque in small additions, stirring all the while. When the rice is just tender, finish with butter.

Plating

On a warm plate, set a ring mold just large enough for a single serving.

Spoon the risotto into the mold, taking care not to pack it too tightly.

Arrange a few slices of lobster on top and spoon some sauce over the top.

Garnish with microgreens and edible flower petals and serve immediately.

Chocolate Fondant with Rum Chocolate Sauce and *Crème Anglaise*

I love this chocolate fondant recipe because it always turns out perfect. I choose the darkest chocolate available, preferably 70% cocoa. Paired with the chocolate sauce and the delicate *crème anglaise*, it becomes a refined, deeply satisfying dessert that's light yet indulgent.

4 servings

INGREDIENTS

Chocolate Fondant

- 5¼ oz. (150 g) bittersweet chocolate
- ⅔ c. (150 g) unsalted butter
- 3 eggs (150 grams)
- ½ c. (100 g) sugar
- ⅓ c. + 1 tbsp. (50 g) all-purpose flour
- Pinch of salt

Chocolate Sauce

- 3½ oz. (100 g) 70% dark chocolate
- ½ c. (100 ml) heavy cream
- ¾ tbsp. (10 g) unsalted butter
- 1½ tbsp. (25 ml) rum

Crème Anglaise

- 2 c. (500 ml) whole milk
- 5 egg yolks (100 g)
- ¼ c. + 1 tbsp. (60 g) granulated sugar
- Vanilla extract, to taste
- Pinch of salt

Garnish

- Edible flowers

PREPARATION

Chocolate Fondant

Whisk the eggs and sugar at medium speed for two minutes.

Melt the chocolate and butter in a saucepan, then stir into the egg mixture.

Slowly add in the flour.

Pour the batter into greased and floured dariole molds.

Bake at 350 °F (175 °C) for 7 to 10 minutes.

Chocolate Sauce

Finely chop the chocolate and place in a mixing bowl.

Heat the cream and rum in a saucepan until just boiling, then pour over the chocolate.

Add thc butter and stir until all of the ingredients are fully melted and the sauce is smooth.

Transfer to a piping bag and set aside.

Crème Anglaise

Cream the egg yolks and sugar until pale.

Heat the milk with the vanilla in a saucepan, then remove from heat.

Gradually whisk the hot milk into the yolk and sugar mixture.

Return to the stove and cook over low heat, stirring continuously, until the custard thickens enough to coat the back of a spoon.

Do not let it boil.

Transfer to a bowl, cover with plastic wrap pressed onto the surface, and chill.

Plating

Brush a line of chocolate sauce across the plate, or alternatively, pipe a few dots of chocolate around the dish.

Carefully remove the fondants from their molds and set each one in the center of a plate on top of the line of sauce.

Garnish with edible flowers, and serve immediately with the *crème anglaise*.

m8

- Crab *Tosta*, Onion Rings
- Asparagus-Wrapped Sea Bass, Hollandaise Sauce
- Braised Kid Goat with Jus and *Tuile* Crisp
- Chocolate and Nut *Turrón*

Chef Enrique Limardo

Driven by a deep passion for the culinary arts, the Venezuelan chef Enrique Limardo has garnered acclaim in the United States, where he serves as partner and executive chef at Imperfecto—a Michelin-starred restaurant since 2022—and at Seven Reasons, hailed as Washington DC's top dining spot. His culinary journey began in Venezuela and continued in Spain, where he trained with acclaimed chefs including Joan Roca, Ramón Freixa, Xavier Pellicer, Joan Piqué, and Carles Gaig. He eventually returned to Caracas to head the kitchens at Paprika and Yantar. His cuisine weaves together Latin and Venezuelan flavors with Mediterranean inspiration—an approach that has captivated countless diners.

Crab *Tosta*, Onion Rings

I prepared this menu inspired by Enrique's dishes, which were served at an exclusive dinner we created together, and by offerings from his former restaurant Yantar in Caracas. This recipe is one of them: a refined, delicate dish—delightful in its play of creamy and crunchy. A light, crisp puff pastry forms the base for a juicy crab mixture, brightened by citrusy mayonnaise that offsets the sweetness of the shellfish. The crisp onion rings bring the perfect finishing crunch—a harmonious contrast of textures and flavors.

4-6 servings

INGREDIENTS

Tosta
- 3½ oz. (100 g) puff pastry
- 2 tbsp. + 1 tsp. (20 g) all-purpose flour
- Salt

Crab Cream
- 8½ oz. (240 g) cleaned crab meat
- ⅓ c. (80 g) mayonnaise
- 2 tsp. (10 g) lemon zest
- Salt
- White pepper

Mayonnaise
- 1¾ c. (400 ml) oil
- 5 egg yolks (100 g)
- 4 tsp. (20 g) Dijon mustard
- 2 tsp. (10 ml) lemon juice
- ¾ tsp. (4 g) salt

Onion Rings
- 1 medium onion
- ⅓ c. (40 g) all-purpose flour
- ½ tsp. (2 g) salt

Garnish
- 1 Granny Smith apple
- Edible flowers
- Microgreens

PREPARATION

Tosta

Roll the puff pastry into a 10 × 8-inch (25 × 20 cm) rectangle about 1⁄16 to ⅛ inch (1–2 cm) thick.
Lay the dough out on a silicone baking mat on top of a baking sheet.
Lightly sprinkle with salt. Cover with another silicone mat and add a light weight on top.
Bake at 320 °F (160 °C) for 20 minutes or until golden brown. Remove from the oven and let cool.
Using a 1½ × 2-inch (4 × 5 cm) cutter as a guide, cut the puff pastry into rectangles with a serrated knife.
Keep dry until serving.

Crab Cream

Combine the crab meat with the mayonnaise, adding the mayonnaise gradually to reach a creamy but firm consistency.
Fold in the lemon zest along with salt and a touch of white pepper.
Chill in the refrigerator for at least 20 minutes to let the flavors develop.

Mayonnaise

Blend the egg yolks, Dijon mustard, and salt in a blender.
With the blender running, drizzle in the oil in a thin stream until the mixture emulsifies and thickens.
Add the lemon juice. Season to taste and set aside.

Onion Rings

Use a mandoline to slice the onion into very thin rings.
Toss the onion rings in a bowl with flour and salt until all the rings are evenly coated.
Fry in oil at 320 °F (160 °C) until crisp and golden.
Remove and season with a bit more salt. Set aside.

Plating

Arrange a puff pastry rectangle on a plate.
Use a rectangular mold to fill the top of the pastry with a ½-inch (1 cm) layer of crab cream.
Place 3 or 4 onion rings on top of the crab cream.
Garnish with julienned green apple.
Add a few microgreens and edible flowers for a final touch.
Serve immediately.

Asparagus-Wrapped Sea Bass with Hollandaise Sauce

This is an elegant presentation, where the fish—with its white, juicy flesh—is wrapped in thin slices of asparagus, giving it a delicate and fresh appearance with a subtle bitterness. The hollandaise sauce, with its buttery flavor and slight tang, enhances the tenderness of the fish and the freshness of the asparagus. This luxurious combination is not only visually appealing but also offers a balanced, light, and delicious bite.

4 servings

INGREDIENTS

Asparagus-Wrapped Sea Bass

- 1½ lb. (650 g) sea bass
- 20 large green asparagus
- 1 tbsp. + 1 tsp. (20 ml) olive oil
- 2 tbsp. (30 ml) heavy cream
- 1 tbsp. (15 g) egg white

Hollandaise Sauce

- 5 egg yolks (100 g)
- 1⅓ c. (300 g) butter
- ¾ c. + 1 tbsp. (200 ml) white wine vinegar
- 4 tbsp. (60 ml) water
- 2 tbsp. + 1 tsp. (20 g) shallots
- Salt
- Lemon juice
- 4 whole peppercorns

Garnish

- Edible flowers
- Microgreens

PREPARATION

Asparagus-Wrapped Sea Bass

Cut four portions of sea bass, each approximately 5½ ounces (150 g), measuring 1¼ × 2½ inches (3 × 6 cm).
Prepare a fish mousse using 1 ounce (30 g) of trimmings from the sea bass.
Blend the fish with cream and egg whites until you obtain a smooth consistency.
Set aside.
Reserve 4 asparagus spears for steaming and use in plating.
Use a vegetable peeler to shave the remaining asparagus into long, thin ribbons.
Place the ribbons in a bowl with a pinch of salt to gently soften.
Spread a sheet of plastic wrap on a large surface.
Weave the asparagus ribbons by alternating horizontal and vertical strips, as if you were weaving a basket, to form a 5-inch (12 cm) square.
Place 1 sea bass portion at the center, slightly toward the bottom edge.
Spoon a thin layer of mousse onto the sea bass.
Carefully wrap the fish with the asparagus ribbons.
Trim off any excess asparagus.
Wrap tightly in plastic wrap, sealing both ends securely.
Set aside.

Hollandaise Sauce

Combine the chopped shallots, white wine vinegar, and peppercorns in a saucepan.
Simmer the mixture until reduced to ¼ cup (60 ml).
Set aside.
Melt the butter over medium heat until the milk solids separate, and strain it through cheesecloth to clarify.
The clarified butter should be golden and completely free of solids.
Set aside.
In a mixing bowl, whisk the egg yolks with the ¼ cup (60 ml) vinegar reduction and ¼ cup (60 ml) water.
Beat vigorously to aerate the mixture.
Place the bowl over a double boiler, making sure it doesn't touch the simmering water.
Whisk the egg yolks continuously, lifting off the heat occasionally to avoid the egg from setting.
Once thick and airy, remove from heat and slowly stream in the clarified butter while whisking constantly.
When fully emulsified, season with salt and a squeeze of lemon to taste.
Set aside.

Asparagus-Wrapped Sea Bass with Hollandaise Sauce

Plating

Steam the wrapped fish for 10 minutes or until a skewer pierces through effortlessly.

Remove from heat.

Gently remove the plastic wrap and transfer to a warmed serving plate.

Add one of the reserved steamed asparagus spears and a spoonful of hollandaise.

Garnish with edible flower petals and microgreens.

Serve immediately.

Braised Kid Goat with Jus and *Tuile* Crisp

This is my version of a stew that yields tender, juicy meat that pulls apart easily when cut. Slow cooking brings out the rich, earthy flavors of the kid goat, and the concentrated juices add a delicious depth. The golden, crispy *tuile* adds a modern contrast that balances the rustic stew with a refined touch.

4 servings

INGREDIENTS

Braised Kid Goat
- 1¾ lb. (800 g) leg of kid goat
- ⅔ c. (100 g) carrot
- ⅔ c. (100 g) onion
- ⅔ c. (100 g) celery
- 1 c. (250 ml) beef stock
- ⅓ c. (40 g) all-purpose flour

Sauce
- ⅔ c. (150 ml) beef stock
- 7 tbsp. (100 g) butter

***Tuile* Crisp**
- 3½ tbsp. (50 g) butter
- ⅓ c. + 1 tbsp. (50 g) all-purpose flour
- 2 egg whites (50 g)
- 1/8 tsp. (0.5 g) salt

Garnish
- Microgreens
- Edible flowers

PREPARATION

Braised Kid Goat

Dice the onion, celery, and carrot into ⅜-inch (1 cm) cubes.

Sauté in a large pot with olive oil until lightly golden.

Remove from heat and season with salt and pepper.

Arrange the kid goat legs on a tray.

Season with salt and pepper.

Dredge the goat pieces in flour and brown on both sides in butter in the same pot used for sautéing vegetables.

After searing, return the meat to the pot together with the vegetables.

Add broth only until it is level with the meat, not fully covering it.

Let cook over medium-low heat for 2–3 hours.

Test tenderness with a knife after cooking, since time varies by piece size and quality.

Once tender, transfer meat and vegetables to a tray. Cover and let rest.

At this stage, debone and portion if desired, or serve bone-in. Set aside.

Sauce

Return the cooking pot to the stove and deglaze with beef broth.

Add 3½ tbsp. (50 g) of butter. Stir until melted and combined.

Strain everything into a separate pot to extract as much liquid as possible.

Adjust salt and butter until the sauce is glossy and coats the back of a spoon. Set aside.

***Tuile* Crisp**

Combine all ingredients until smooth.

Spread the mixture in a *tuile* mold into the desired shape.

Bake in a preheated oven at 350 °F (175 °C) for 5 minutes.

Plating

Heat some of the sauce in a deep pan.

Place the kid goat pieces to be served in the pan and spoon sauce over to heat.

Spoon a generous amount of sauce into a warmed shallow bowl.

Arrange 2 pieces of the kid goat in the bowl. Add 3 cubes each of carrot and celery.

Drizzle more warm sauce over the meat and vegetables.

Top with the *tuile* crisp.

Garnish with edible flower petals and microgreens.

Serve immediately.

Chocolate and Nut *Turrón*

I have included this dessert as I felt that chocolate would be the perfect finishing touch to elegantly close the meal. This delicious *turrón* blends the rich complexity and intense flavor of chocolate with the crunchy texture of toasted nuts delivering a sweet, pleasurable bite that offers a perfect final note to conclude the menu.

6-8 servings

INGREDIENTS

Chocolate and Nut *Turrón*
- 14 oz. (400 g) dark chocolate
- 2 tbsp. (30 g) butter
- 2 tbsp. (30 g) sweetened condensed milk
- ½ c. (75 g) hazelnuts
- ½ c. (75 g) almonds
- ½ c. (75 g) walnuts
- ½ c. (75 g) pistachios

Chocolate Cream
- ½ c. (100 ml) heavy cream
- 3½ oz. (100 g) chocolate

Topping
- 3½ oz. (100 g) chocolate couverture
- Edible flowers

PREPARATION

Chocolate and Nut *Turrón*

Toast the nuts in the oven at 250 °F (120 °C) for 10 to 15 minutes, until golden.

Finely chop the toasted nuts and set aside.

Melt the chocolate with the butter in the microwave, heating for 30-second intervals and stirring each time to avoid burning the chocolate.

Stir in the nuts and condensed milk.

Mix until all ingredients are fully combined.

Transfer the mixture into individual silicone molds.

Another option is to line a rectangular mold with plastic wrap and press the mixture in gently with a spatula.

Press lightly to shape the mixture evenly.

Allow to cool completely until firm.

Chocolate Cream

Heat the cream and fold in the chopped chocolate until it melts.

Stir continuously until the mixture is smooth and uniform.

Transfer to a piping bag and set aside.

Topping

Finely chop the remaining chocolate coverture into small bits.

Transfer to a bowl and melt over a double boiler.

Spread a thin 1 mm layer of chocolate onto an acetate sheet.

When it begins to crystallize but before it hardens, cut into 4 × ¾-inch (10 × 2 cm) rectangles.

Set aside and let set completely.

Plating

Gently remove the *turrón* from the mold.

Cut the *turrón* into different shapes, including ¾-inch (2 cm) squares and ¾ × ½-inch (2 × 1 cm) rectangles.

Arrange the pieces on a rectangular plate or small tray.

Pipe small dots of chocolate cream to one side.

Garnish with a chocolate sheet and edible flowers.

Serve immediately.

- Spherified Olives with Anchovy and Red Pepper Pearls
- Prawn Ravioli with Mushrooms, Leek *Velouté*, and Orange Gel
- Lamb Couscous with Jus, Red Pepper Salad, Chickpeas
- Mascarpone Sphere with Chocolate, Crispy *Tuile*

Chef Eduardo Moreno

From his first bistro, Blue Moon, and his Moroccan venture Vlassis Le Med, self-taught chef Eduardo Moreno has continually surprised guests with his diverse offerings, such as molecular cuisine. As a child, he remembers being inspired in the kitchen by his French grandmother. Today, in addition to consulting for various culinary venues in Venezuela, he hosts an intimate tasting experience at his home in Caracas, La Isabela.

Spherified Olives with Anchovy and Red Pepper Pearls

This book would not be complete without a molecular cuisine menu—especially spherifications. I made a few changes to the original recipe and prepared two versions instead of one. The first is the liquid olive, with its fluid center that gently bursts in the mouth when bitten. The second is a bell pepper spherification that pairs beautifully with the olive, creating a more complex and playful flavor. Both preparations are examples of innovative culinary techniques that transform traditional ingredients into unique and surprising gastronomic experiences.

6-8 servings

INGREDIENTS

ANCHOVY-STUFFED LIQUID OLIVES

Olive Juice

- 14 oz. (400 g) pitted green olives
- ¾ c. + 1 tbsp. (200 ml) olive brine
- 2 tbsp. + 2 tsp. (40 ml) lemon juice

Olive Mixture

- 1¾ c. (400 ml) olive juice (see preparation below)
- 1/11 (0.09) oz. (2.5 g) calcium chloride

Spherified Olives with Anchovy

- 1¾ cups (500 ml) water
- 1/11 (0.09) oz. (2.5 g) alginate
- 1 small can (1.8 oz. / 50 g) anchovies packed in oil
- Olive mixture (see preparation below)

Miscellaneous

- 1 tbsp. (10 g) Maldon salt
- 6-8 thinly sliced toasted baguette rounds
- Microgreens

PREPARATION

Olive Juice

Purée the green olives using an immersion blender, gradually incorporating their brine and the lemon juice.

Strain the juice and refrigerate.

Olive Mixture

Combine the olive juice and calcium chloride with an immersion blender.

Allow to rest.

Spherified Olives with Anchovy

Use an immersion blender to mix the water and alginate until fully dissolved.

Transfer to a bowl.

Prepare a second bowl with cold, clean water.

Spoon out some of the olive mixture, insert a sliver of anchovy, and drop into the alginate solution.

Let the sphere form and set for 4 minutes.

Gently lift out with a slotted spoon and transfer to the cold water to rinse.

Drain thoroughly and store in a glass jar filled with olive oil.

Keep refrigerated.

Spherified Olives with Anchovy and Red Pepper Pearls

INGREDIENTS
RED PEPPER PEARLS

- 14 oz. red bell peppers (400 g)
- ⅓ c. (80 ml) extra virgin olive oil
- Salt

Red Pepper Mixture

- 1¾ c. (400 ml) red pepper purée (see below)
- ⅓ (0.09) oz. (2.5 g) calcium chloride

Red Pepper Spherification

- 2 c. (500 ml) water
- 1/11 (0.09) oz. (2.5 g) alginate
- Red pepper mixture (see below)

PREPARATION

Red Pepper Purée

Place the peppers on a baking sheet, drizzle with a little olive oil, and place in the oven.

Roast for 2 hours at 350 °F (175 °C), or until soft and wrinkled.

Remove from the oven, place in a bowl, and cover with plastic wrap.

Allow to rest for 1 hour.

Peel and seed the peppers, then transfer the peppers along with their juices to a glass container.

Purée the peppers with some of their juices, adding salt to taste and more olive oil if needed to reach a smooth, slightly fluid consistency.

Strain the purée through a fine sieve and set aside.

Red Pepper Mixture

Blend the pepper purée and calcium chloride with an immersion blender.

Allow to rest.

Red Pepper Spherification

Use an immersion blender to mix the water and alginate until fully dissolved.

Transfer to a bowl.

Prepare a second bowl with cold, clean water.

Spoon out some of the pepper mixture and drop into the alginate solution.

Let the sphere form and set for 4 minutes.

Gently lift out with a slotted spoon and transfer to the cold water to rinse.

Drain thoroughly and store in a glass jar filled with olive oil.

Keep refrigerated.

Plating

Place a liquid olive sphere on a ceramic tasting spoon.

Add a sphere of liquid red pepper alongside.

Garnish with a touch of Maldon salt and a single microgreen.

Accompany with a paper-thin slice of toasted baguette.

Prawn Ravioli with Mushrooms, Leek *Velouté*, and Orange Gel

This dish is a blend of refinement and finesse. The ravioli, made from thin prawn sheets and filled with a mushroom *duxelles*, strike a refined balance between marine and earthy flavors. The silky leek *velouté* offers depth, thanks to its mild sweetness and herbal notes. The orange gel finishes the dish with a citrusy freshness and a bright, glossy accent

4 servings

INGREDIENTS

Prawn Ravioli
- 8 large prawns
- Maldon salt

Mushroom *Duxelles*
- 1 lb. (500 g) mushrooms
- 3½ tbsp. (50 ml) sunflower oil
- 1 small onion (about 4 oz. / 120 g)
- 3½ oz. (100 g) fresh parsley
- ¼ tsp. (1 ml) truffle oil

Leek Broth
- 1 c. + 2 tbsp. (150 g) leek
- ¾ c. (100 g) chives
- ⅓ c. (50 g) carrot
- 3½ tbsp. (50 ml) olive oil
- 1¾ cups (400 ml) water

Leek *Velouté*
- 1¼ c. (280 ml) leek broth
- 1 tbsp. (15 g) butter
- 2 tbsp. (15 g) all-purpose flour
- Salt
- Black pepper

Orange Gel
- ¾ c. (175 ml) orange juice
- 2 tbsp. (25 g) sugar
- ½ tsp. (2 g) agar-agar

Garnish
- Microgreens
- Edible flowers

PREPARATION

Prawn Ravioli

Peel the raw prawns and freeze them for 2 hours.

Take them out 15 minutes before serving.

Place the prawns between two sheets of acetate.

Gently flatten them with a mallet until they form a ⅛-inch (2 mm) sheet.

Patch any empty spots to ensure a full sheet.

Return to the freezer to set.

Mushroom *Duxelles*

Dice the mushrooms into ⅛-inch (3 mm) cubes.

Finely dice the onion and sauté it in sunflower oil until golden.

Stir in the mushrooms and brown for a few more minutes.

Add finely chopped parsley to the pan and mix well.

Finish with a splash of truffle oil.

Set aside.

Leek Broth

In a large pot, sauté the leek, chive, and diced carrot in olive oil.

Add the water when the vegetables are well browned.

Bring to a boil, then reduce the heat.

Let the broth reduce by two-thirds.

Strain the broth and set aside.

Leek *Velouté*

Make a roux in a small saucepan.

Melt the butter and whisk in the flour, stirring constantly for 2 to 3 minutes until it smells slightly nutty.

Take off the heat and add one-third of the leek broth, whisking to prevent lumps.

Add the rest of the broth, bring to a boil, and simmer while stirring until it thickens slightly.

Prawn Ravioli with Mushrooms, Leek *Velouté*, and Orange Gel

Adjust salt to taste.
Strain the *velouté* through a fine sieve and set aside.

Orange Gel
Blend all the ingredients in a saucepan.
Bring to a boil, stirring constantly.
Pour the mixture into a tray.
Place plastic wrap directly on the surface to prevent a skin from forming.
Chill in the fridge for about 2 hours until set.
Remove from tray and blend until smooth and glossy.
Transfer to a small squeeze bottle or piping bag.
Set aside.

Plating
Remove the frozen prawn sheet and cut into 8 squares.
Lay each square on a piece of plastic wrap.
Add 1 tablespoon of the *duxelles* in the center of 4 squares.
Top each one with a second square to form a raviolo and seal tightly with plastic wrap.
Unwrap the ravioli and place in a shallow bowl.
Heat the bowl in the oven for 1 minute.
Pour the previously heated *velouté* evenly over the plate, as a base, forming a smooth mirror.
Add a few drops of olive oil to the *velouté*.
Dot each raviolo with a few drops of orange gel.
Garnish with microgreens and edible flowers.
Finish with a sprinkle of Maldon salt.
Serve immediately.

Lamb Couscous with Jus, Red Pepper Salad, Chickpeas

Lamb couscous is one of the most iconic dishes of Moroccan cuisine, where lamb takes center stage. The original recipe was more heavily spiced and sweet; mine is more French in style, like what my grandmother and later my mother used to make. If desired, you can add turmeric, cumin, or other spices to the vacuum bag. In this dish, the couscous acts as a light and fluffy base—the perfect texture for absorbing the lamb juices. The cooked red pepper salad, with its natural sweetness and subtle smokiness, adds a distinct touch to the dish. Finally, chickpeas are a cornerstone of Moroccan cuisine, not only for their mildly earthy and neutral flavor, but also because they are an iconic ingredient that symbolizes abundance and hospitality.

4-6 servings

INGREDIENTS

Lamb Shank

- 2¼ lb. (1 kg) lamb shank or leg
- ⅓ c. + 1 tbsp. (100 ml) olive oil
- 2 garlic cloves
- ¾ tsp. (3 g) salt
- ½ tsp. (2 g) black pepper
- 3 tbsp. (40 g) butter

Couscous

- ⅔ c. (160 g) precooked couscous
- 1 c. + 2 tbsp. (280 ml) vegetable broth
- 3 tbsp. (40 g) butter

Cooked Chickpeas

- 18 oz. (500 g) dry chickpeas
- 2 c. (500 ml) beef broth
- Water
- Salt

Red Pepper Salad

- 1¾ lb. (800 g) red bell pepper
- 9 oz. (250 g) peeled tomatoes
- 4 tbsp. (60 ml) olive oil
- 1 garlic clove
- Salt

Garnish

- Edible flowers

PREPARATION

Lamb Shank

Vacuum-pack the lamb shank with the marinade of olive oil, whole garlic (germ removed), salt, and black pepper.

Cook in a controlled-temperature water bath at 158 °F (70 °C) for 24 hours.

Remove from the bath after cooking is complete and chill quickly in an ice bath to 37 °F (3 °C) in under 2 hours.

Keep the vacuum bag refrigerated until ready to serve.

About an hour before serving, warm the lamb in a water bath for 20 minutes, until the juices are fully liquefied and the meat feels warm.

Carefully snip the corner of the bag and pour the cooking juices into a saucepan.

Remove the lamb from the bag and transfer to a serving platter, covering with foil to keep warm.

Couscous

Heat the vegetable broth and the butter in a saucepan until just boiling.

Add the couscous.

Cover and remove from the heat.

Let stand, covered, for 5 to 6 minutes.

Fluff gently with a fork, making sure all the liquid has been absorbed.

Set aside.

Cooked Chickpeas

Soak the chickpeas in water the day before.

Drain the chickpeas the next day and discard the soaking water.

Cook the chickpeas in a pot with the broth over medium heat until tender.

Set aside.

Lamb Couscous with Jus, Red Pepper Salad, Chickpeas

Red Pepper Salad

Rub the red peppers with olive oil and place on a baking tray.

Roast in the oven at 350 °F (175 °C) for 2 hours, or until very soft and the skins have browned and blistered.

Transfer to a bowl and cover with plastic wrap until cool.

Peel the peppers and remove stems and seeds.

Slice into long strips about ¼ inch (½ cm) thick.

Likewise, slice the peeled tomatoes into long strips.

Heat some of the olive oil in a deep frying pan.

Add the whole garlic clove and stir until golden brown.

Remove the garlic and add the peeled tomato.

Cook for about 4 minutes, then add the sliced peppers.

Add salt and simmer on low for 2 hours until the flavors are concentrated.

Turn off the heat and keep covered.

Set aside.

Plating

Reheat the lamb juices in a saucepan.

Add the chickpea broth and bring to a boil.

Lower the heat slightly and reduce until the mixture is brothy.

In a hot, deep frying pan, add the lamb and a bit of the broth.

Baste the meat continuously to warm it through.

Plate the lamb and garnish with a few flower petals.

Serve the couscous, the red pepper salad, and the chickpeas in separate bowls.

Accompany with the lamb broth in a sauce boat.

Serve immediately.

Mascarpone Sphere with Chocolate, Crispy *Tuile*

In this recipe, I replaced the traditional tiramisu with a more modern adaptation that combines luxury and contrasting textures. These are delicate chocolate spheres whose crisp exterior breaks open to reveal a creamy mascarpone center. The *tuile* adds a crunchy texture and a hint of caramelization that complements the smoothness of the mascarpone and the chocolate.

4-6 servings

INGREDIENTS

Mascarpone Cream
- 1 c. (250 g) mascarpone cheese
- 1¾ c. (400 ml) heavy cream
- 4 egg yolks (80 g)
- ¾ c. (150 g) sugar
- ½ tsp. vanilla extract

Tuile
- 7 tbsp. (100 g) unsalted butter
- ½ c. (100 g) sugar
- 3 egg whites (100 g)
- ¾ c. + 2 tbsp. (100 g) all-purpose flour

Chocolate Shell
- 10½ oz. (300 g) couverture chocolate

Garnish
- ½ c. (50 g) cocoa powder
- Edible flowers

PREPARATION

Mascarpone Cream

Whisk the egg yolks with the sugar until pale, and the mixture doubles in volume.
In a separate bowl, soften the mascarpone, then fold in the yolk mixture.
In another bowl, whip the heavy cream with the vanilla until it holds stiff peaks.
Carefully fold the whipped cream into the mascarpone mixture.
Transfer to a piping bag.
Keep chilled until needed.

Chocolate Shell

Finely chop the chocolate into small bits.
Transfer to a bowl and melt over a double boiler.
Use a pastry brush to coat the inside of silicone half-sphere molds with the chocolate.
Repeat with 2 or 3 layers of chocolate until the desired thickness is obtained.
Let the chocolate set completely before using.

Mascarpone Sphere

When the chocolate shells are firm, fill them with the chilled mascarpone cream.
Wipe away any excess and freeze for a minimum of 4 hours, until the filling is frozen.

Tuile

Preheat the oven to 350 °F (175 °C).
Gently melt the butter, without overheating.
Combine the flour, sugar, and egg whites, then add the melted butter.
Mix until smooth.
Spread a thin layer of the batter into a silicone *tuile* mold, smoothing with a spatula for clean edges.
Bake for 4–6 minutes or until golden and easily released from the mold.
Gently lift the *tuile* from the mold and allow it to cool completely.

Plating

Remove the mascarpone spheres from their molds while still frozen.
Arrange on the serving dish and let sit a few minutes to soften slightly.
Use a fine sieve to dust the spheres with cocoa powder.
Gently place a *tuile* on top of each sphere.
Garnish with edible flowers and serve immediately.

m10

- Foie Gras Creams, Blueberry *Gelée*, Blueberry Gel
- Sous-Vide Confit Pork, Teriyaki Sauce, Basmati Rice, Smoked Hazelnut Mayonnaise
- Caramelized Apple Crisp in Two Cooking Techniques

Chef Eduardo Moreno

From his first bistro, Blue Moon, and his Moroccan venture Vlassis Le Med, self-taught chef Eduardo Moreno has continually surprised guests with his diverse offerings, such as molecular cuisine. As a child, he remembers being inspired in the kitchen by his French grandmother. Today, in addition to consulting for various culinary venues in Venezuela, he hosts an intimate tasting experience at his home in Caracas, La Isabela.

Foie Gras Creams, Blueberry *Gelée*, Blueberry Gel

I completely reworked this recipe while preserving foie gras as the central ingredient. For me, this dish is an explosion of color and flavor. The velvety and indulgent foie gras cream balances sweet and savory with the distinct mineral nuance of foie. The gleaming blueberry gel adds brightness and fruitiness, lifting the richness of the liver with a tart contrast. The blueberry *gelée* delivers a punch of fruit flavor in a light, gelatin texture that balances the creaminess and subtle earthiness of the foie. This dish is served with toasted brioche for the perfect accompaniment.

4 servings

INGREDIENTS

Foie Gras Cream
- 5 oz. (140 g) foie gras pâté
- 1 c. (250 ml) heavy cream
- 1⅓ c. (200 g) blueberries
- 4 egg yolks (80 g)
- 2 sheets gelatin
- 1 tsp. (5 g) salt

Blueberry *Gelée*
- 3½ tbsp. (50 ml) blueberry juice
- 3½ tbsp. (50 ml) honey
- 1 sheet gelatin
- 1 tsp. (5 ml) water

Blueberry Gel Glaze
- 1 c. less 1 tbsp. (225 ml) blueberry juice
- 1 tbsp. (15 ml) balsamic vinegar
- Pinch of salt
- 1¼ tsp. (3.5 g) powdered kappa carrageenan

Garnish
- Edible flowers
- Microgreens
- Blueberries

PREPARATION

Blueberry *Gelée*

Heat the blueberry juice with the honey.
Add the previously bloomed and melted gelatin sheet.
Pour a 1/16-inch (2 mm) layer into half of the square molds for the foie gras.
Transfer to the refrigerator and chill until set.

Foie Gras Cream

Bloom the gelatin in cold water.
In a saucepan, combine the cream, egg yolks, and salt.
Whisk thoroughly and cook over medium heat, stirring constantly, until thickened.
Remove from the heat and stir to cool slightly.
Add the gelatin and foie gras.
Use an immersion blender to blend until creamy and well emulsified.
Strain into a bowl and let cool to room temperature.
Transfer to a piping bag and fill various molds in the shape of hemispheres and squares.
Fill the molds containing the set blueberry *gelée* as well.
Tap gently to release any trapped air bubbles.
Press 1 blueberry into each shape, making sure it is completely encased, like a filled chocolate.
Freeze until firm.

Blueberry Gel Glaze

Blend all the ingredients in a saucepan using an immersion blender, then heat until fully combined.
Pour into a wide-mouthed container.
Unmold half of the foie gras creams.
Pierce each foie gras mousse with a thin wooden skewer and dip it into the glaze to form a thin layer of blueberry gel.
Place on a tray and let cool until set.
Set aside.

Foie Gras Creams, Blueberry *Gelée*, Blueberry Gel

Plating

Place one mousse of each type on a plate: one plain, one with the gel glaze, and one with the *gelée* base.

Feel free to combine different shapes.

Garnish with edible flowers, microgreens, and blueberries.

Serve.

Sous-Vide Confit Pork, Teriyaki Sauce, Basmati Rice, Smoked Hazelnut Mayonnaise

While I adapted some elements of this dish, its essence remains: a celebration of technique and flavor. The pork is slow-cooked at a low temperature, resulting in a very tender, silky texture, while retaining all its natural juices. The teriyaki sauce is a recipe I developed during the pandemic. It is simple and delicious, with sweet and savory notes that envelop the pork in an irresistible umami flavor. The basmati rice serves as a neutral canvas that balances the dish's bold flavors, while the hazelnut mayonnaise brings creaminess and sophistication, with a gently toasted and subtly smoky note.

4 servings

INGREDIENTS

Sous-Vide Confit Pork
- 1 leg of pork
- 3 tsp. (10 g) coarse salt
- 2 tsp. (10 g) sugar
- Olive oil
- 1 tbsp. (5 grams) fresh oregano

Teriyaki Sauce
- ⅓ c. + 1 tbsp. (100 ml) soy sauce
- ⅓ c. + 1 tbsp. (100 ml) mirin
- ⅓ c. + 1 tbsp. (100 ml) sake
- ⅓ c. + 1 tbsp. (100 ml) balsamic vinegar
- ⅓ c. + 1 tbsp. (100 ml) vegetable or chicken broth
- ¼ c. (50 g) sugar
- 1 oz. (30 g) piece fresh ginger
- 1 tbsp. (10 g) cornstarch (optional)

Basmati Rice
- 1 c. (200 g) basmati rice
- 1¾ c. (400 ml) water
- 1 tsp. (5 g) salt
- 1 tbsp. + 1 tsp. (20 ml) sunflower oil

Hazelnut Mayonnaise
- 1 egg (50 g)
- 1 egg yolk (20 g)
- Sunflower oil
- ⅓ c. (50 grams) hazelnuts
- ½ tsp. (2 g) salt

Garnish
- Toasted hazelnuts
- Microgreens and fresh greens
- Edible flowers

PREPARATION

Sous-Vide Confit Pork

Rub the pork leg with the mixture of coarse salt and sugar.
Let rest on a tray for 45 minutes.
Rinse off the salt, then vacuum-pack with olive oil and oregano.
Cook sous vide for 24 hours at 162 °F (72 °C) in a controlled water bath.
Remove from the bath and chill quickly to 34 °F (3 °C) in under 2 hours.
Keep chilled.
When ready to plate, return the bag with the meat to a hot water bath for about 15 minutes.
Open the bag carefully, making sure not to lose any of the cooking juices.
Remove the meat and cut into 1¼-inch (3 cm) squares.
Keep the pork moist by storing it covered with the strained cooking liquid.

Teriyaki Sauce

Combine all the liquids, sugar, and finely grated ginger in a small saucepan.
Simmer over medium heat until reduced by a third or until it reaches a syrupy consistency.
If needed, add cornstarch to thicken slightly.
Set aside.

Basmati Rice

Heat the oil in a saucepan.
Add the rice and stir for 1 minute.
Add the water and salt.
Stir and bring to a boil.
Once boiling, reduce heat to medium until some of the water is absorbed.
Cover and simmer on low for 3 to 4 minutes, until the rice is cooked through but still firm and the water has been absorbed. Set aside.

Sous-Vide Confit Pork, Teriyaki Sauce, Basmati Rice, Smoked Hazelnut Mayonnaise

Hazelnut Mayonnaise

Toast the hazelnuts in the oven at 280 °F (140 °C) on a silicone-lined tray for about 15 minutes, or until golden brown.

Place the whole egg and the yolk in a blender or immersion blender container.

Add the salt and blend on medium speed.

Slowly drizzle in the oil until a stable, creamy emulsion forms.

Add the toasted hazelnuts and continue blending, or grind with the immersion blender.

Adjust salt to taste, transfer to a piping bag, and set aside.

Plating

Arrange two separate pieces of pork on a rectangular plate and brush with teriyaki sauce.

Mold the rice using small ring molds and alternate with the pork pieces.

Make small dots of hazelnut mayonnaise and others with teriyaki sauce.

Garnish with halved toasted hazelnuts, fresh greens, microgreens, and edible flower petals.

Serve immediately.

Caramelized Apple Crisp in Two Cooking Techniques

In this dessert, I once again use only the main ingredient from the original recipe: apples. The idea is to create a light yet more sophisticated dessert. It begins with the delicacy of phyllo dough, with its light and crispy texture. The apples are prepared two ways: one remains tender yet firm, with a warm sweetness; the other is thinly sliced and caramelized, offering a visual contrast and a deeper flavor. This is elevated with a touch of cream—soft and barely sweetened—which balances the textures and adds a creamy element that ties all the components of the dessert together.

4 servings

INGREDIENTS

Apples, Technique 1
- 3 Granny Smith apples
- ⅓ c. (75 g) sugar
- 3½ tbsp. (50 g) butter

Apples, Technique 2
- 3 Granny Smith apples
- 2 tsp. (55 g) sugar
- 2 tbsp. (30 g) butter

Phyllo Pastry
- 10½ oz. phyllo dough (300 g)
- ⅔ c. (150 g) butter

Whipped Cream
- ¾ c. + 1 tbsp. (200 ml) heavy cream
- 2 tsp. (10 g) sugar

Garnish
- Fresh mint leaves
- Edible flowers

PREPARATION

Apples, Technique 1
Peel and core the apples.
Dice the apples into small cubes.
Melt the butter in a frying pan, then add the sugar and diced apples.
Cook for a few minutes until golden, without letting the apples lose their shape.
Set aside.

Apples, Technique 2
Peel and core the apples.
Slice them into ¹⁄₁₆-inch (2 mm) slices using a mandoline.
Grease a 4 × 8-inch (10 × 20 cm) rectangular loaf pan with butter.
Sprinkle with sugar and layer the apple slices, one on top of the other, to cover the base and reach a height of at least ¾ inch (2 cm).
Cover with aluminum foil, pressing it directly onto the apples.
Place another mold or a weight on top.
Bake at 350 °F (175 °C) for 1 hour.
Remove from the oven and let cool.
Invert the mold and carefully turn the apples out.
Cut into rectangles measuring 1 × 2 inches (2.5 × 5 cm).
Set aside.

Phyllo Pastry
Melt the butter.
Unroll the phyllo dough.
On a flat surface, place one sheet of phyllo and brush with melted butter.
Add a second sheet and repeat the process until you have 5 layers.
Cut into 1 × 2-inch (2.5 × 5 cm) rectangles and arrange on a baking sheet lined with a silicone mat.
Place a second silicone mat on top of the rectangles.
Bake at 350 °F (175 °C) for 10 minutes or until golden.
Store in a cool, dry place.

Caramelized Apple Crisp in Two Cooking Techniques

Whipped Cream

Beat the heavy cream with sugar until stiff peaks form.

Transfer to a piping bag and set aside.

Plating

Place one piece of baked phyllo pastry on a plate.

Add one rectangle of sliced apples on top.

Add a second layer of phyllo pastry.

Carefully spoon the diced apples on top and distribute evenly.

Add a third layer of pastry and pipe a few dots of whipped cream on top.

Finish with a final layer of phyllo pastry, and garnish with a few dots of whipped cream, fresh greens, and edible flowers.

Serve immediately.

m11

- Ceviche *Limeño*, Calamari Rings
- Tuna *Tiradito*, Popcorn, *Ají Amarillo*
- Seafood Ceviche, Sweet Potato Spheres, *Ají Rojo*
- Fruit Ceviche, Blackberry Coulis

Chef Víctor Moreno

A familiar face in the Venezuelan media, chef Víctor Moreno began his career in the kitchen at the age of sixteen. He later pursued formal training at CEGA (Centro de Estudios Gastronómicos) in Caracas, where he was awarded a scholarship to study in Spain. While there, he worked at El Racó de Can Fabes under Santi Santamaría, and at Balzac, with Andrés Madrigal. From there, he moved on to Peru, working at El Señorío del Sulco, and then to Mexico and Colombia before returning to CEGA as executive chef. He was a founding partner and executive chef of the now-closed Moreno, named Venezuela's best restaurant in 2023 by The World Culinary Awards. He is currently the culinary director at Menta y Romero.

Ceviche *Limeño*, Calamari Rings

Ceviche is a classic of Peruvian cuisine; however, here I wanted to add a touch of originality by combining the freshness of ceviche with the crispness of calamari in a single dish. It is a simple dish that highlights the clean flavor of the fish, balancing acidity with the subtle heat of the chili. The calamari, with its crispy coating, gives way to a tender and juicy texture that perfectly offsets the intensity of the ceviche. The accompaniment of yellow chili paste intensifies the chili's flavor, while the sautéed sweet potato adds a mellow sweetness that contrasts perfectly with the citrus and spice.

4-6 servings

INGREDIENTS

Ceviche *Limeño*
- 1¾ lb. (800 g) white fish (sea bass, snook, or red snapper)
- ¾ c. (100 g) red onion
- ½ c. (80 g) *ají amarillo* (yellow chili pepper)
- ⅓ oz. (10 g) cilantro
- 1½ c. (360 ml) lemon juice
- Salt

Calamari Rings
- 14 oz. (400 g) calamari tubes
- Flour
- Salt
- Wooden skewers

Garnish
- Edible flower petals
- Cilantro microgreens

Accompaniment
- 2 medium-sized (12 oz. / 350 g) sweet potatoes

***Ají* Paste**
- 2⅔ c. (400 g) *ají amarillo* (yellow chili pepper)
- 3½ tbsp. (50 ml) water
- ¼ c. (60 ml) neutral oil

PREPARATION

Ceviche *Limeño*

Julienne the red onion and soak in a bowl with ice. Set aside.

Thinly slice the *ají amarillo* and finely chop the cilantro. Set aside.

Squeeze the lemon juice and set aside.

Brunoise dice the fish into ⅛-inch (1.5 cm) cubes.

Mix the fish with salt in a bowl and let it sit for a few minutes.

Remove the onion from the ice and dry it thoroughly with a paper towel.

Combine the fish with the onion, sliced *ají*, and chopped cilantro.

Add the lemon juice.

Stir gently to combine, then cover and refrigerate.

Calamari Rings

Slice the cleaned calamari tubes into 1⁄16-inch (2 mm) rings.

Place the rings in a bowl and dust generously with flour to coat.

Heat the oil in a pot.

Shake off any excess flour and fry the calamari at 195 °F (90 °C) until golden brown.

Set aside.

Accompaniment

Brunoise dice the sweet potato into ⅛-inch (2 cm) cubes.

Cook the sweet potatoes in boiling water until just tender.

Sauté the sweet potatoes in a nonstick frying pan with a bit of oil until just golden.

Set aside.

***Ají Amarillo* Paste**

Slice the *ajíes* in half lengthwise. Carefully remove the seeds and veins, avoiding contact, as this is the spiciest part.

Place the *ají* in a pot with cold water and bring to a boil.

Once boiling, discard the water and start again with fresh water.

This process can be repeated 2 or 3 times if desired to reduce the heat of the peppers.

Ceviche *Limeño*, Calamari Rings

Peel the chilies and blend, then slowly add the oil and water to form a smooth, creamy paste, as you continue to blend.

Set aside.

Plating

Remove the ceviche from the refrigerator.

Stir again to recombine and adjust seasoning if needed.

In a deep bowl, place one tablespoon of ceviche with a bit of *leche de tigre* (marinade juice).

Garnish with flower petals and cilantro microgreens.

Skewer a few calamari rings on a wooden pick long enough to balance on the edges of the bowl.

Balance the skewer over the ceviche.

Accompany with sautéed sweet potatoes and yellow *ají* paste.

Serve immediately.

Tuna *Tiradito*, Popcorn, *Ají Amarillo*

This dish began as a ceviche, but I chose to transform it into a tiradito, which I personally find better suited to tuna. The thin slices highlight the vibrant ruby-red color and allow the natural sweetness, acidity, and subtle heat of the ají sauce to come through evenly. The creamy avocado lends smoothness, and the crunchy, lightly salted popcorn offers a delightful and unexpected crunch.

4-6 servings

INGREDIENTS

Tuna *Tiradito*

- 1¾ lb. (800 g) sushi-grade tuna loin
- ¾ c. (100 g) red onion
- ⅓ c. + 1 tbsp. (50 g) *ají amarillo* (yellow chili pepper)
- ⅓ oz. (10 g) cilantro

***Ají Amarillo* Sauce**

- 1½ c. (200 g) *ají amarillo* (yellow chili pepper)
- ⅓ c. + 1 tbsp. (100 ml) lemon juice
- 5 tbsp. (70 ml) oil
- ⅓ c. (40 g) celery
- 1 garlic clove

Accompaniment Popcorn

- ½ c. (100 g) popcorn kernels
- 3½ tbsp. (50 ml) neutral oil

Sweet Potato Purée

- 1½ to 2 medium (14 oz / 300 g) sweet potatoes

Avocado Cream

- 1⅓ c. (200 g) avocado
- 2 tsp. (10 ml) lemon juice
- Salt

Garnish

- Edible flowers
- Cilantro microgreens
- Chives

PREPARATION

Tuna *Tiradito*

Place the tuna loin in the freezer for 1 hour for easier slicing.

Cut the tuna into 1/16-inch (2 mm) thick slices and lay them side by side on a piece of plastic wrap to form a large rectangle.

Cover with a second layer of plastic wrap.

Set the wrapped tuna on a board or tray and freeze until solid.

Brunoise dice the red onion and thinly slice the *ají amarillo*. Set aside.

Finely chop the cilantro and set aside.

***Ají Amarillo* Sauce**

Slice the *ajíes* in half lengthwise. Carefully remove the seeds and veins, avoiding contact, as this is the spiciest part.

Place the *ajíes* in a pot with cold water and bring to a boil.

Once boiling, discard the water and start again with fresh water.

This process can be repeated 2 or 3 times if desired to reduce the heat of the peppers.

Peel the chilies and blend, then slowly add the oil and water to form a paste.

Add the celery and the clove of garlic with the germ removed.

Continue to blend, then slowly add the lemon juice to form a smooth, creamy paste.

Transfer to a squeeze bottle and set aside.

Popcorn

Heat the oil in a small saucepan with a lid.

Add the popcorn kernels and cover immediately.

Remove from the heat once the popping has stopped.

Transfer to a bowl, season with salt, and set aside.

Sweet Potato Purée

Arrange the sweet potatoes on a baking sheet.

Rub the sweet potatoes with oil and roast at 350 °F (175 °C) for 1 hour, or until easily pierced with a knife.

Tuna *Tiradito*, Popcorn, *Ají Amarillo*

Peel the sweet potatoes and blend with a pinch of salt until smooth.
Transfer to a piping bag and set aside.

Avocado Cream

Blend the avocado flesh with lemon juice and salt until thick and creamy.
Transfer to a piping bag and set aside.

Plating

Remove the tuna from the freezer and, using a sharp knife, cut into 2 × 5-inch (5 × 12 cm) rectangles.
Peel off the top layer of plastic wrap and invert onto a plate.
Carefully peel off the remaining plastic wrap.
Garnish the tuna with rings of *ají amarillo*, diced red onion, and cilantro, and top with a few dots of *ají amarillo* sauce.
Add a few dots of avocado cream and sweet potato purée on top.
Crumble the popcorn and sprinkle it over the tuna.
Garnish with microgreens, edible flower petals, and chives.
Serve immediately.

Seafood Ceviche, Sweet Potato Spheres, *Ají Rojo*

This ceviche is an explosion of freshness, flavor, and color evoking the warmth of the tropics and the richness of the sea. The seafood includes calamari, octopus, and shrimp but can be replaced with mussels or any other fresh shellfish. While the sweet touch comes from the cooked and caramelized sweet potato, a tropical fruit like mango could also be used, adding color and natural sweetness.

4-6 servings

INGREDIENTS

Seafood Ceviche

- 1 lb. (500 g) calamari
- 1 lb. (500 g) shrimp
- 1 lb. (500 g) octopus
- 3½ oz. (100 g) cilantro
- ¾ c. (100 g) red onion
- 1 c. (240 ml) lemon juice
- 1 c. (150 g) *ají dulce* (sweet chili pepper)
- ¾ c. (100 g) *ají amarillo* (yellow chili pepper)
- Salt
- Black pepper

Accompaniment

- 1½ to 2 medium (14 oz. / 400 g) sweet potatoes
- 3 tbsp. (40 g) butter
- 1 tbsp. + 1 tsp. (20 g) sugar
- Salt
- Sriracha or spicy red chili sauce

Garnish

- Micro arugula
- Edible flower petals

PREPARATION

Calamari

Lay the cleaned calamari flat on a board to form rectangles.

Make shallow crisscross diagonal cuts, being careful not to cut through the calamari, and boil in a pot of salted water for 1 to 2 minutes.

Keep chilled until needed.

Shrimp

Peel and clean the shrimp.

Boil the shrimp in a pot of salted water for 1 to 2 minutes, depending on the size.

Keep chilled until needed.

Octopus

Dip the cleaned octopus once into a deep pot of boiling, lightly salted water, holding it by the head with a pair of tongs, then remove.

Repeat this process 3 times, then cook for 25 minutes or until tender when pierced with a knife.

Keep chilled until needed.

Seafood Ceviche

Slice the prepared calamari into ⅜-inch (1 cm) rings.

Cut the shrimp into ⅜-inch (1 cm) pieces.

Cut off the octopus tentacles and slice into ⅜-inch (1 cm) medallions.

Dice the rest of the octopus into ⅜-inch (1 cm) cubes.

Keep chilled until needed.

Julienne the red onion and place in a bowl with ice.

Set aside.

Thinly slice the *ají amarillo* and set aside.

Finely chop the cilantro and set everything aside.

In a large bowl, combine all the seafood with the onion, ajíes, cilantro, and lemon juice, stirring briskly.

Let it marinate in the fridge for 10 minutes.

Adjust salt to taste.

Seafood Ceviche, Sweet Potato Spheres, *Ají Rojo*

Accompaniment

Boil the sweet potatoes in a pot of salted water until tender but still firm.

Drain and let cool.

Peel the sweet potatoes and use a small *Parisienne* (⅜ inch / 1 cm) to scoop out spheres of potato.

Place the butter and sugar in a non-stick pan.

Allow the sugar to melt, then add the sweet potato.

Add a pinch of salt, and sauté for a few minutes until glossy and caramelized.

Set aside.

Plating

Spoon a serving of the seafood ceviche into a shallow bowl.

Add three or four spheres of sweet potato.

Dot with spicy *ají rojo* sauce.

Garnish with micro arugula and edible flower petals.

Serve immediately.

Fruit Ceviche, Blackberry Coulis

This menu originally did not include dessert, but in keeping with the theme of chilled, light ceviches and tiraditos, what better way to close than with a colorful, refreshing take on these iconic dishes with a tropical twist? The charm of this recipe lies in the detail of the fruit cuts—geometric shapes in small circles, squares, and triangles. The blackberry coulis adds sweetness and elegance, elevating the dish with both color and gourmet appeal.

4-6 servings

INGREDIENTS

Fruit Ceviche
- 2 c. (300 g) papaya
- 2 c. (300 g) watermelon
- 2 c. (300 g) cantaloupe
- 1¾ c. (250 g) pineapple
- 1½ c. (200 g) strawberries
- 1½ c. (200 g) raspberries
- 1½ c. (200 g) grapes
- 1 orange
- 1 banana
- 2 tbsp. (30 ml) lemon juice
- 3½ tbsp. (50 ml) orange juice

Blackberry Coulis
- 1¼ c. (150 g) blackberries
- ¼ c. + 2 tbsp. (75 g) sugar
- 3½ tbsp. (50 ml) water

Garnish
- Fennel sprigs or mint leaves

PREPARATION

Fruit Ceviche

Peel the papaya and remove the seeds.

Scoop out balls of papaya using a parisienne scoop and set aside.

Cut the rind from the watermelon and remove the seeds.

Scoop out balls of watermelon using a parisienne scoop and set aside.

Cut the rind from the cantaloupe and remove the seeds.

Scoop out balls of cantaloupe using a small parisienne scoop and remove the seeds.

Cut the rind from the pineapple and slice into ⅜-inch (1 cm) thick rounds.

Cut the rounds into ⅜-inch (1 cm) cubes and set aside.

Slice the strawberries lengthwise into quarters and set aside.

Slice the raspberries in half and set aside.

Peel the grapes, slice in half, and set aside. Set aside.

Peel the orange, removing all white pith. Segment the orange into supremes.

Peel the banana and slice into ⅜-inch (1 cm) cubes. Set aside.

On a glass tray, arrange the papaya, watermelon, melon, pineapple, grapes, and orange supremes. Pour the lemon juice and orange juice over the fruit.

Tilt the tray gently to let the juices coat the fruit evenly, without using a spoon.

Keep chilled until needed.

The strawberries, raspberries, and banana should not be macerated in the juice to preserve their form and texture. Chill these fruits separately.

Blackberry Coulis

Bring the blackberries and the water to a boil in a small saucepan.

Strain through a fine sieve to extract all the pulp.

Return the pulp to the pot and heat with the sugar.

Simmer over low heat until it reaches a syrup-like consistency.

Let cool and transfer to a squeeze bottle.

Plating

Arrange the sliced fruit on one side of the plate, alternating colors and shapes.

Add a few spheres of fruit of varying sizes to form a crescent.

Pipe a few dots of blackberry coulis on either side of the fruit.

Garnish with a few sprigs of fennel or a few fresh mint leaves. Serve chilled.

m12

- Vichyssoise, Herb *Île Flottante*
- Prawn Ravioli, Lettuce Jus
- Herb-Crusted *Carré d'agneau*, Glazed Carrots, *Mousseline* Purée
- Tarte Tatin, the Classic and the Contemporary

Chef Thierry Mugnier

The French chef Thierry Mugnier, owner of the restaurant Le Genépi in Courchevel, France, has worked in some of the most prestigious restaurants in his country and is a member of the Association of Young Restaurateurs of France. Throughout his career, he has refined his skills in the kitchens of notable European establishments, including the Martinez in Cannes and the Hotel du Palais in Biarritz, prior to establishing his own restaurant, Le Genépi, in 1994. Mugnier is characterized by his innovative approach to cuisine, in which he uses local and seasonal ingredients in his dishes.

Vegetable Vichyssoise, Herb *Île Flottante*

Vichyssoise could be considered the French equivalent of gazpacho—a cold soup primarily containing potatoes, leeks, and cream, typically enjoyed in the summer. This recipe was essential for this book because vichyssoise is the base for many other French soups, and has the added advantage of being served hot or cold, depending on the season.

4 servings

INGREDIENTS

Vichyssoise
- ¾ c. (100 g) celery stalks
- ¾ c. (100 g) fennel
- 1¼ c. (180 g) potatoes
- 2 c. (300 g) leeks (white part only)
- 1½ zucchini
- 1¼ c. (300 ml) chicken stock
- 3½ tbsp. (50 g) heavy cream
- Olive oil
- Salt
- Black pepper

Herb *Île Flottante*
- 2 large egg whites
- ⅔ c. (50 g) chives

Garnish
- Chives
- Microgreens
- Edible flowers

PREPARATION

Vichyssoise

Dice the celery, fennel, potatoes (all but one), and leeks (all but one).

Sauté in olive oil, together with the sliced zucchini, for 5 minutes without browning.

Add the potatoes and chicken stock.

Bring to a boil and cook for 30 minutes.

Add salt and pepper to taste.

Purée for 3 minutes to obtain a smooth, soup-like consistency.

Strain through a fine-mesh sieve.

Stir in the cream and allow to cool.

Use a parisienne scoop to make small spheres with the remaining potato, cook in boiling water until tender, then set aside with a drizzle of olive oil.

Slice the remaining leek into ⅝-inch (1.5 cm) rounds, then boil in a bit of salted water, taking care not to let it fall apart.

Set aside.

Herb *Île Flottante*

Beat the egg whites to soft peaks.

Using an ice cream scoop, form a ball with the beaten egg whites.

Gently poach in boiling water for 2 minutes. Carefully lift out.

For a contemporary plating, use a cylindrical cutter to shape the floating island.

The chives may be sprinkled atop the floating island or folded into the mixture.

Plating

Pour the chilled vichyssoise into a shallow bowl, then center a cylinder of the herb *île flottante* on top.

Add a few potato spheres and two small bits of cooked leek.

Garnish the *île flottante* with chives, and the soup with edible flowers and microgreens.

Serve immediately.

Prawn Ravioli, Lettuce Jus

This ravioli dish is quite distinct, fresh, and full of flavor. Here, I used wonton wrappers instead of preparing the pasta (though I've included the recipe). Wonton wrappers are thinner and more elastic, making them very easy to fill and shape. The original recipe featured a whole prawn, but for this version it was cut smaller and seasoned like a tartare so that once cooked, it would be more flavorful and have a softer, more delicious texture. The lettuce jus is remarkably fresh and pleasant, with a subtly sweet taste that perfectly complements the marine flavor of the prawn.

4-6 servings

INGREDIENTS

Ravioli Dough

· 14 sheets wonton wrappers

Dough (if wonton wrappers are unavailable)

· 1⅔ c. (200 g) all-purpose flour

· 3 large eggs

· 1 tbsp. (15 ml) olive oil

· Salt

· 1 tbsp. + 1 tsp. (20 ml) water

Filling

· 12 to 16 prawn tails (caliber 16/20)

· Olive oil

· Salt

· Black pepper

Sauce

· 1 leaf vibrant green lettuce

· ⅔ c. (150 ml) white chicken stock

· 3 tbsp. (40 g) butter

· Salt

· Black pepper

Garnish

· Microgreens or parsley

PREPARATION

Prawn Filling

Peel and finely dice the prawns.

Add olive oil, salt, and pepper, and set aside.

Ravioli Dough

Add all ingredients except the water to the bowl of a stand mixer. Mix well to combine.

Slowly add the water while mixing until the dough is firm and uniform.

Wrap the dough in wax paper or parchment paper. Let rest in a cool place for 2 hours.

Roll out the dough as thinly as possible, 1/16 inch (1–2 mm) thick.

Cut into 4-inch (10 cm) rounds or squares.

Ravioli

Place one tablespoon of the prawn mixture in each circle or square of dough, moisten the dough around the filling, and cover with another circle or square, pinching the edges to seal.

Arrange the assembled ravioli on a lightly oiled baking sheet.

Keep chilled until ready to serve.

Lettuce Jus

Quickly blanch the lettuce in boiling salted water, then immediately chill in an ice bath.

Drain and blend with the chicken stock. Adjust salt and pepper to taste. Set aside.

Plating

For serving, bring a large pot of salted water with a touch of oil to a boil.

Cook the ravioli for 2 or 3 minutes and drain.

At the same time, heat the butter until it releases a nutty aroma, always being careful to prevent burning.

Heat the lettuce jus.

Ladle 2 tablespoons of lettuce jus into the bottom of the dish, then arrange 3 or 4 raviolis on top.

Drizzle 2 teaspoons of browned butter over each raviolo.

Garnish and serve immediately.

Herb-Crusted *Carré d'Agneau*, Glazed Carrots, *Mousseline* Purée

This is a dish that everyone enjoys because it combines the juiciness and tenderness of the lamb with the freshness and aroma of the herbs. The herb crust—in this case, parsley, chives, and garlic—adds an unparalleled burst of flavor to the meat. If desired, rosemary, thyme, or other herbs can be added as well. This is a dish of great culinary elegance and refined flavor, perfect for a special occasion.

4 servings

INGREDIENTS

Carré d'Agneau

- 2 racks of lamb (ask for 2 extra bones separately)
- 1 tbsp. + 1 tsp. (20 ml) oil
- 1 tbsp. (15 g) butter
- 1 medium onion
- 1 carrot
- 1 sprig thyme
- 1 bay leaf
- 4 garlic cloves
- Salt
- Black pepper

Herb Crust

- ⅔ oz. (20 g) flat-leaf parsley
- ⅔ c. (20 g) chives
- 7 tbsp. (100 g) butter
- 2 slices (100 g) sandwich bread
- 3 garlic cloves
- Salt
- Black pepper

Glazed Carrots and Onions

- 1 c. (150 g) baby carrots
- 4 pearl onions
- Sugar
- 2 tbsp. (30 g) butter
- 1 tbsp. oil
- Salt
- Black pepper

Potato Mousseline

- 1 lb. (500 g) potatoes
- ¾ c. + 1 tbsp. (200 ml) heavy cream
- ½ c. + 1 tbsp. (125 g) butter
- 1 tsp. (5 g) salt

Garnish

- Edible flowers
- Microgreens

PREPARATION

Carré d'Agneau

Heat the oil and butter and quickly brown the racks of lamb on all sides.

Season with salt and pepper.

Remove the lamb and transfer it to a baking tray.

Sauce

Place the extra bones from the racks of lamb on a baking sheet and roast in the oven until golden.

Peel and chop the onion and garlic.

Peel and slice the carrots.

Add the carrots, onion, garlic, thyme, and bay leaf to the browned bones.

Pour in 4¼ cups (1 l) of water and cook in the oven for one hour.

This should yield nearly 3 tablespoons (40 ml) of sauce.

Herb Crust

Prepare the crust while the sauce is cooking in the oven.

Crumble the bread, cut the butter into pieces, and blend in a food processor for 2 minutes.

Add the finely chopped herbs and the peeled, minced garlic.

Season with salt and pepper and blend again.

Using a rolling pin, spread this mixture between two sheets of wax paper or parchment paper and chill in the refrigerator.

Glazed Carrots and Onions

Boil the carrots for a few minutes in a pot of salted water, drain, and immediately transfer to a bowl of ice water.

Herb-Crusted *Carré d'Agneau*, Glazed Carrots, *Mousseline* Purée

In a pan, melt 1 tablespoon (15 g) of butter with 1 teaspoon of sugar and a pinch of salt; add the carrots and 2 tablespoons of water.

Cook over low heat; the carrots will be ready once the water evaporates.

In another pan, prepare the onions in the same way.

Potato *Mousseline*

Wash the potatoes well and place them in a pot.

Cover with water and bring to a boil.

Once cooked, peel the potatoes and press them through a potato ricer.

Transfer the puréed potatoes to a pot and reheat, stirring constantly with a spatula.

Add the cold butter, cut into small cubes, and mix well.

Gradually add the cream while stirring to obtain a thick purée consistency.

Season with salt.

Transfer to a piping bag and set aside.

Carré d'Agneau

Cut 2 squares of the herb crust to the size of the fat on the racks of lamb, and cover the fat with the crust.

Bake at 400 °F (210 °C) for 10 minutes.

Cut the racks of lamb into double chops.

Plating

Place two pairs of ribs on a preheated plate.

Add some carrots and onions and pipe a few dots of potato *mousseline* onto the plate.

Garnish with edible flower petals and microgreens.

Serve immediately with a little sauce.

Tarte Tatin, the Classic and the Contemporary

Tarte tatin is a classic of French gastronomy and has become an iconic dessert. Its charm lies in the fact that it is baked upside-down and flipped to serve. Although traditionally made with apples, it can also be prepared with pears or other fruits. Typically a rustic tarte, my contemporary version takes on a refined and elegant character by delicately slicing the apples before caramelizing and baking.

6-8 servings

INGREDIENTS

Tarte Tatin

· 10 Granny Smith apples
· 1 c. less 2 tbsp. (200 g) butter
· 1 c. (200 g) sugar
· Puff pastry

Whipped Cream

· 2 c. (500 ml) heavy cream
· ½ c. (100 g) sugar
· 2 tbsp. + 2 tsp. (40 ml) Calvados

PREPARATION

Classic Tarte Tatin

Peel the apples and cut in half.

In a 12-inch (30 cm) oven-safe dish or individual molds, add the dry sugar and heat until a golden caramel is obtained. Add the butter in pieces and the halved apples.

If using the large dish, arrange the apples in a circle, finishing with the center.

If using individual molds, place one half apple in each mold, cut side up.

Bake at 300 °F (150 °C) for 30 minutes.

Allow to cool slightly.

For the 12-inch (30 cm) tart, cut the puff pastry disc about ¾ inch (2 cm) larger to seal around the apples.

For individual molds, cover with a puff pastry disc the same size as the mold.

Return to the oven and bake at 400 °F (210 °C) for 10 minutes or until golden brown.

Contemporary Tarte Tatin

Apples

Peel the apples.

Using a fruit and vegetable slicer similar to the KitchenAid attachment, slice the apple by rotating it to obtain the thinnest possible slices.

Once all the apples are sliced, roll them into spirals of various diameters for the large version, or all the same diameter for the individual molds.

Trim the spirals to the same height.

In a square 8-inch (20 cm) baking dish or individual molds, prepare a caramel with the sugar.

Add the butter in pieces and arrange the apple spirals in the molds.

If using the large mold, alternate large and small spirals, filling in the gaps with smaller rolls made from leftover slices.

If using individual molds, place 1 apple spiral in each.

Bake at 300 °F (150 °C) for 20 to 30 minutes, depending on size, until golden.

Remove from oven and allow to cool slightly.

Puff Pastry

Roll out the puff pastry, sprinkling powdered sugar as you go until it reaches a thickness of ⅛ inch (3 mm).

Chill in the refrigerator for a few minutes.

Lay out the pastry on a silicone mat on a baking sheet, place another mat on top, and gently set another tray on top of the mat to keep it flat.

Bake at 350 °F (175 °C) for 25 minutes.

Once golden, and at room temperature, cut an 8-inch (20 cm) square for the large version, or circles to match the mold size for individual portions.

Return to the oven and bake at 400 °F (210 °C) for 10 minutes or until golden brown.

Whipped Cream

Whip the cream to soft peaks, then add the sugar and Calvados.

Plating

Invert the tart and unmold onto a serving plate.

Serve with whipped cream on the side.

m13

- Turkey and Pistachio Terrine, Onion Marmalade
- *Foie Gras Poêlé aux Pommes et Raisins*
- *Bar Rôti,* Fennel-Tomato, *Beurre Blanc*
- Crème Brûlée, Crisp Caramel

Chef Thierry Mugnier

The French chef Thierry Mugnier, owner of the restaurant Le Genépi in Courchevel, France, has worked in some of the most prestigious restaurants in his country and is a member of the Association of Young Restaurateurs of France. Throughout his career, he has refined his skills in the kitchens of notable European establishments, including the Martinez in Cannes and the Hotel du Palais in Biarritz, prior to establishing his own restaurant, Le Genépi, in 1994. Mugnier is characterized by his innovative approach to cuisine, in which he uses local and seasonal ingredients in his dishes.

Turkey and Pistachio Terrine, Onion Marmalade

The terrine is a classic French dish that showcases a balance of textures and flavors. For this version, I chose turkey and pistachios. The original version called for hazelnuts, but pistachios bring a vibrant green tone that enhances the visual appeal. Their mild sweetness pairs beautifully with the turkey and gives a smoother, more delicate texture compared to hazelnuts.

8 servings

INGREDIENTS

Turkey Terrine
- 1 whole turkey
- ⅓ c. (50 g) carrot
- ⅓ c. (50 g) onion
- ⅓ c. (50 g) leek
- 1 sprig thyme
- 1 bay leaf
- 1 c. (150 g) shelled pistachios
- Salt
- Black pepper

Onion Marmalade
- 2 lb. 3 oz. (1 kg) onions
- 3½ tbsp. (50 g) butter
- 3 c. (750 ml) red wine
- ½ c. (100 g) sugar

Lettuce Garnish with its Vinaigrette
- 10 oz. (250 g) mesclun mix
- ⅓ c. + 1 tbsp. (100 ml) walnut oil
- 2 tbsp. sherry vinegar
- 1 tbsp. whole grain mustard
- Salt
- Black pepper

PREPARATION

Turkey Terrine

Debone the turkey.

Weigh out 2 lb. 3 oz. (1 kg) of meat and 1 lb. 5 oz. (600 g) of bones.

Cut the meat into slices ¼ inch (5 mm) thick and about 1¼ inches (3 cm) long.

Season the meat with 4 teaspoons (20 g) of salt and ¾ teaspoon (3 g) of pepper.

Keep chilled until needed.

Prepare a turkey stock: peel the carrots, onions, and leek.

Add to a pot with the turkey bones, thyme, and bay leaf.

Add enough water to cover and bring to a boil over high heat.

Skim regularly and reduce until only 1 cup (250 ml) of stock remains.

Strain the stock and let cool until it becomes gelatinous.

Finely chop the pistachios and mix them with the turkey meat.

Add the gelatinized stock.

Transfer the mixture into a terrine mold, arranging the turkey pieces lengthwise, and add the pistachio-stock mixture so it distributes evenly between the layers.

Cover and cook in a double boiler for 1 hour in the oven at 340 °F (170 °C).

Let cool and refrigerate the terrine overnight.

Onion Marmalade

Peel the onions and slice into julienne strips.

Sauté gently over high heat with butter until lightly golden.

Add the red wine and sugar. Reduce until all the liquid has evaporated. Let cool.

Vinaigrette

Mix the vinegar with the mustard, salt, and pepper.

Slowly add the oil while whisking to form an emulsion. Set aside.

Plating

Slice the terrine and arrange one slice per plate.

Spoon a portion of onion jam on top of the terrine.

Serve with a handful of mesclun.

Drizzle a little vinaigrette over the greens and serve.

Foie Gras Poêlé aux Pommes et Raisins

Foie gras is a globally renowned delicacy and a cornerstone of French gastronomy. Its flavor is smooth and unique, and although pairing it with apple is classic, I find it to be a perfect match. The acidity and freshness of the apple, along with the natural sweetness of both the apple and green grape, contrast beautifully with the richness and fattiness of the foie gras—resulting in a balanced and delicious experience.

4 servings

INGREDIENTS

Foie Gras

- 1 foie gras (18 oz. / 500 g)
- 1 tbsp. flour

Apples and Grapes

- 4 Golden Delicious apples
- 1 bunch green grapes
- 2 tbsp. (30 g) butter

Sauce

- ¾ c. (150 g) sugar
- ¾ c. + 1 tbsp. (200 ml) Port wine
- ¾ c. + 1 tbsp. (200 ml) veal, chicken, or beef stock
- 2 tbsp. (25 g) potato starch
- 2 tbsp. (50 g) butter
- Salt
- Black pepper

Garnish

- Microgreens

PREPARATION

Foie Gras

Cut the foie gras into 8 slices, each about ⅝ inch (1.5 cm) thick.

Remove the veins using the tip of a knife, then season both sides of each slice with salt and pepper.

Apples and Grapes

Peel the grapes and remove the seeds.

Peel the apples. Using a small parisienne scoop, scoop out small spheres, or thinly slice the apples lengthwise, removing the core and seeds.

Melt 2 tablespoons (30 g) of butter in a frying pan and brown the apples on all sides.

Keep warm.

Sauce

Cook the sugar in a small saucepan until it becomes lightly caramelized.

Add the Port wine and stir gently with a rubber spatula.

Mix the chicken stock with the potato starch and add it to the caramel. Reduce.

Add 50 g of butter in small pieces, stirring continuously.

Taste and adjust the seasoning as needed.

Stir the grapes into the sauce.

Warm the sauce for 2 minutes.

Set aside.

Plating

Lightly flour the foie gras slices and sear them for 1 to 2 minutes on each side in the same pan used for the apples.

Arrange the foie gras on warm plates, and surround each piece with the sautéed apples and grapes. Spoon the sauce over the foie gras, garnish with microgreens, and serve immediately.

Bar Rôti, Fennel-Tomato, *Beurre Blanc*

I used snapper for this version, known for its moist, white flesh, complemented here by fennel and sautéed tomatos for a fresh and subtly sweet balance. While the original version featured preserved lemon and fava bean sauce, I opted for *beurre blanc*—an elegant and delicious sauce that is emblematic of French cuisine and also one of my personal favorites. Its texture is smooth and creamy, and it pairs perfectly with the fish.

4 servings

INGREDIENTS

Bar Rôti

- 4 white fish fillets (grouper, sea bass, or snapper), 5¼ oz. (150 g) each, skin on
- 2 tbsp. + 2 tsp. (40 ml) olive oil

Fennel-Tomato

- 4 small tomatoes
- 2 c. (300 g) fennel
- 1 onion
- 4 tbsp. (60 ml) olive oil
- 1½ tbsp. (20 g) butter
- Salt
- Black pepper

Beurre Blanc

- 3½ tbsp. (50 ml) white wine
- 1½ tbsp. (25 ml) white wine vinegar
- 3 tbsp. (30 g) shallot
- 3½ tbsp. (50 ml) heavy cream
- 1 c. less 2 tbsp. (200 g) butter
- Salt
- Black pepper

Garnish

- Edible flowers
- Microgreens

PREPARATION

Bar Rôti

Arrange the fish fillets on a tray.

Season both sides with salt and pepper, and set aside to cook just before plating.

Fennel-Tomato

Peel the onion and cut into julienne. Trim the fennel, removing the stalks and base.

Cut the bulb into fine slices.

Peel and seed the tomatoes, and cut into thin julienne strips.

Sauté the onion and fennel gently in 2 tablespoons (30 ml) of olive oil for 10 minutes.

Season with salt and pepper to taste.

Stir the tomatoes into the cooked onion and fennel.

Sauté for just a few minutes longer, only until the tomatoes begin to soften.

Sauce

Combine the white wine, vinegar, and chopped shallots in a small saucepan over medium heat.

Simmer until reduced to a syrupy consistency—about 2 to 3 tablespoons.

Stir in the cream and season with salt and pepper.

Allow the mixture to boil gently for 1 minute.

Reduce the heat to very low.

Begin whisking in cold butter, a few cubes at a time.

Keep adding butter gradually before each addition is fully melted.

Lift the pan off the heat now and then to keep the temperature low; the final texture should be like hollandaise sauce.

Set aside and keep warm for serving.

Plating

Warm 2 tablespoons (30 ml) of olive oil in a frying pan.

Sear the fillets skin-side down for 6 to 7 minutes.

Turn the fillets over and cook briefly on the other side.

Remove from heat.

Spoon 2 tablespoons of the fennel-tomato mixture onto a preheated plate.

Lay the fish on top of the vegetables, skin-side up.

Add a few microgreens and spoon the *beurre blanc* around the fish. Serve immediately.

Crème Brûlée, Crisp Caramel

Crème brûlée is a beloved staple of French desserts—I couldn't omit it. The original recipe used *pain d'épice*, a French spice bread flavored with cinnamon, clove, anise, and other warm spices. I'm not a fan of clove or overly spiced mixes, so I opted for a simple vanilla infusion. Of course, the flavor profile can be customized by infusing the dairy with your preferred aromatics. I also gave it a distinctive touch with the caramel garnish, which makes the plating more appealing, achieving a perfect combination between the creamy texture of the crème brûlée and the crunch of the caramel.

4 servings

INGREDIENTS

Crème Brûlée

- 1 c. (250 ml) heavy whipping cream
- 1 c. (250 ml) whole milk
- 6 egg yolks (120 g)
- 1 vanilla bean
- ½ c. + 2 tbsp. (120 g) sugar
- Pinch of salt
- Sugar for caramelizing, as needed

Caramel Garnish

- ¾ c. (150 g) sugar
- 2 tbsp. water

PREPARATION

Crème Brûlée

In a saucepan, bring the cream, milk, and the scraped vanilla bean (pod and seeds) to a boil.
Take off the heat immediately and allow to infuse for 2 to 3 minutes.
Discard the vanilla pod.
Whisk the egg yolks and sugar together until pale and light.
Combine the egg yolk mixture with the cream and milk, stirring slowly to avoid bubbles.
Strain the custard through a fine-mesh sieve, using a wooden spoon to help it through.
Pour the custard into 4 ramekins, each holding 5–7 ounces (150 to 200 ml).
Bake in a water bath in a preheated 350 °F (175 °C) oven for about 35 minutes.
Remove from the oven and let cool at room temperature.
Refrigerate for 2 to 3 hours before serving.

Caramel Garnish

Combine the sugar and water in a small saucepan.
Cook over medium heat, without stirring.
Gently swirl the saucepan just to moisten the sugar and ensure it cooks evenly.
Watch closely as bubbles form—the caramel will begin to take on color.
Take off the heat once the caramel turns a deep amber.
Use a spoon or a stick to shape the caramel into your desired design on a silicone mat.
Allow the caramel to cool and then gently remove the shapes.

Plating

Right before serving, sprinkle a fine layer of sugar on each custard and caramelize the top using a kitchen torch.
Garnish with the caramel figures and edible flower petals.
Serve immediately.

m14

- Prawns with Artichoke in Four Textures
- White Fish Tartare, Salmon Gravlax and its Coral
- Beef Cheek in Red Wine Sauce, Polenta Fries
- *Tarte au Citron*

Chef Thierry Mugnier

The French chef Thierry Mugnier, owner of the restaurant Le Genépi in Courchevel, France, has worked in some of the most prestigious restaurants in his country and is a member of the Association of Young Restaurateurs of France. Throughout his career, he has refined his skills in the kitchens of notable European establishments, including the Martinez in Cannes and the Hotel du Palais in Biarritz, prior to establishing his own restaurant, Le Genépi, in 1994. Mugnier is characterized by his innovative approach to cuisine, in which he uses local and seasonal ingredients in his dishes.

Prawns with Artichoke in Four Textures

For this version of the recipe, I added a fourth dimension to the artichoke: the flower. In contrast to the original recipe, which featured only three textures of this ingredient, the addition of the artichoke flower brings a touch of elegance, beauty, and refined flavor to the dish. The inspiration comes from an exquisite creation by Albert Adrià: *Artichoke Sunflower with Tarama and Ginger Tapioca*, renowned for its perfect and sophisticated presentation. Each cooking technique contributes a distinct texture and flavor, resulting in an exceptional combination with the prawns.

4 servings

INGREDIENTS

Prawns

· 12 large prawns

Artichoke in Four Textures

· 3 large artichokes

· 8 purple artichokes

· 1 sprig cilantro

· ¾ c. + 1 tbsp. (200 ml) white wine

· Salt

· Black pepper

· Olive oil

Garnish

· Edible flowers

PREPARATION

Artichoke Purée

Steam 3 large artichokes for 1 hour.

Peel and remove the inner filament.

Mash the artichoke flesh with the back of a fork and combine with half of the chopped cilantro.

Season with salt and pepper, and stir in 4 tablespoons of olive oil.

If lumpy, give it a quick blend using a hand mixer or immersion blender.

Sautéed Artichoke Hearts

Trim and peel 2 of the purple artichokes.

Quarter the hearts and sauté them in olive oil until tender.

Season with salt, pepper, and the remaining chopped cilantro.

Deglaze with the white wine, then cover and simmer over low heat for 30 minutes. Set aside.

Artichoke Flower

Take 4 more purple artichokes and trim the tops of the leaves, leaving about ½ inch (1 cm) in height.

Hollow out the center with a spoon, being careful to leave the heart intact.

Make incisions around the leaves, spaced 1/16 inch (2 mm) apart.

Place each prepared artichoke in lemon water to prevent browning.

Pat dry thoroughly and fry in oil until golden and fully cooked.

Drain on paper towels and set aside.

Artichoke Chips

Slice the remaining 2 artichokes finely and fry at 350 °F (175 °C) until golden and crispy.

Set aside.

Prawns

Peel and devein the prawns.

Sear them in hot olive oil for about 3 minutes.

Season with salt and pepper to taste.

Plating

Place an artichoke flower on a plate and add a spoonful of purée. Arrange two pieces of the sautéed artichoke and add a few artichoke chips. Place three sautéed prawns, garnish with a few edible flowers, and serve immediately.

White Fish Tartare, Salmon Gravlax and its Coral

In this recipe, I focused mainly on the presentation and adjusted the seasoning of the fish. It's a dish full of freshness and flavor. The gravlax is delicate and aromatic, while the tartare delivers an explosion of fresh flavors and textures. This time, I paired it with a squid ink coral *tuile*, which wasn't part of the original recipe and adds a unique touch—making the dish more modern and visually playful.

4 servings

INGREDIENTS

White Fish Tartare
- 1 lb. 2 oz. (500 g) raw white fish
- 1 sprig cilantro
- 1½ tbsp. (20 g) capers
- 1½ tbsp. (20 g) gherkin
- 1½ tbsp. (20 g) shallot
- Salt
- Black pepper
- 1½ tbsp. (25 ml) lemon juice
- 1 tsp. Tabasco
- Olive oil

Salmon Gravlax
- 2 lb. 3 oz. (1 kg) fresh salmon
- 1 tbsp. + 1 tsp. (20 ml) lemon juice
- ¾ c. + 1 tbsp. (200 ml) olive oil
- Sugar
- Salt
- Black pepper
- 1 sprig fresh dill

Squid Ink Coral
- ⅓ c. (80 ml) water
- 1 tbsp. + 1 tsp. (20 ml) extra virgin olive oil
- 1 tbsp. (10 g) type 00 flour
- 1 tsp. (4 g) squid ink

Cream
- ⅓ c. (80 g) sour cream
- 1½ tbsp. (25 ml) lemon juice
- Salt
- Black pepper

PREPARATION

White Fish Tartare
Clean the fish thoroughly, removing all skin and pin bones.
Cut the fish into tiny ⅛-inch (3 mm) dice.
Finely mince the shallots, capers, gherkins, and cilantro, then mix with the fish.
Stir in 4 tablespoons olive oil, the lemon juice, Tabasco, salt, and pepper.
Let marinate in the refrigerator for 2 hours.

Salmon Gravlax
Place the cleaned salmon loin in a glass container.
Add a generous amount of salt and sugar, and a touch of pepper on top of the fillet.
Add the lemon juice and the olive oil.
Marinate in the refrigerator for 12 to 18 hours.

Squid Ink Coral
Combine all the ingredients.
Spoon 1 tablespoon of the mixture into a hot frying pan.
The coral will take shape as the water evaporates.
Gently lift it and transfer to a paper towel. Set aside.

Cream
Combine the sour cream, salt, pepper, and lemon juice in a bowl. Set aside.

Plating
To serve, remove the salmon from the marinade, dry thoroughly, and cut into ¾-inch (2 cm) cubes.
Place several cubes of salmon and a few sprigs of dill on the plate.
Filter a little of the marinade and drizzle a few drops over the salmon.
Shape the tartare inside a ring mold on the opposite side of the plate.
Garnish with a squid ink coral and a few small dollops of cream.
A small bowl of extra cream may be served on the side if desired.
Serve immediately.

Beef Cheek in Red Wine Sauce, Polenta Fries

This recipe features a particular cut of beef: the cheek, known as *carrillera* or *carrillada*, which comes from the animal's face. It is a type of meat that requires long cooking times, but it becomes incredibly tender and juicy. If it doesn't feel soft at the end of the cooking time, it can easily be left to cook a bit longer. The red wine–based sauce is widely used in French cuisine, as it brings depth and flavor. The higher the quality of the wine, the more complex and delicious the sauce will be. In addition to offering an appealing visual contrast, the polenta fries served with this dish provide a crispy element, distinguished by a soft and creamy interior. They complement the richness of the beef cheeks and their sauce beautifully.

4 servings

INGREDIENTS

Beef Cheek in Red Wine Sauce

- 1 lb. 12 oz. (800 g) fresh, cleaned beef cheek
- 4¼ c. (1 l) red wine
- 1¾ oz. (50 g) dehydrated veal stock
- 1¾ c. (250 g) carrots
- 1 onion
- 1 bouquet garni with parsley, thyme, and bay leaf

Polenta Fries

- 1 c. (200 g) polenta
- ¾ c. (100 g) all-purpose flour
- 2 c. (500 ml) whole milk
- 4¼ c. (1 l) water
- Salt
- Black pepper
- 7 tbsp. (100 g) butter

Garnish

- Microgreens

PREPARATION

Beef Cheek in Red Wine Sauce

Marinate the beef cheek the day before with red wine, the bouquet garni, onion, and 1 cup (150 g) of finely diced carrot.

Drain the beef cheeks and season generously.

Arrange in a roasting pan, add the red wine and veal stock, and top up with water.

Bring to a boil and then transfer to the oven at 420 °F (215 °C) for 2 hours and 30 minutes, basting every 15 minutes.

Remove the cheeks from the sauce and keep warm.

Strain the sauce and reduce until nappe consistency.

Adjust salt and pepper to taste.

Polenta Fries

Boil the water and milk together, then add salt, pepper, and the polenta.

Simmer over low heat for 30 minutes, stirring occasionally.

Pour the mixture into a tray and let cool for 2 hours.

Cut the polenta into ¾ × ¾ × 4-inch (2 × 2 × 10 cm) sticks, dust with flour, and lightly fry in some butter.

Plating

Cut the cheeks into thick slices and arrange on a warm plate.

Spoon the sauce over the meat.

Add two pieces of fried polenta alongside.

Garnish with a few microgreens and serve immediately.

Tarte au Citron

This lemon tartlet recipe is simply delicious and is a real crowd pleaser. A classic dessert that, in broad terms, brings together the vibrant acidity of lemon with the sweetness and creaminess of the meringue and the tart shell. The base is a *pâte brisée* that melts in the mouth, filled with a lemon cream of intensely citrusy yet balanced flavor. It is finished with meringue which, beyond adding a layer of flavor and texture, lends that touch of sweetness that perfectly complements the acidity of the dessert.

6-8 servings

INGREDIENTS

Pâte Brisée **(Shortcrust Pastry)**

· 1¼ c. (150 g) all-purpose flour
· ⅓ c. (75 g) butter
· ¼ c. (50 g) sugar
· Pinch of salt
· 1 egg yolk
· Water

Lemon Cream

· 1 c. (250 ml) lemon juice
· 5 eggs (250 g)
· 1 c. less 2 tbsp. (200 g) butter
· 1 c. (200 g) sugar
· 2 tbsp. (20 g) potato starch

Meringue

· 3 egg whites (100 g)
· 1 c. (200 g) sugar
· 3 tbsp. (40 g) powdered sugar

Garnish

· Edible flowers

PREPARATION

Pâte Brisée **(Shortcrust Pastry)**

It's best to prepare the dough the day before.
Take the butter out of the refrigerator 15 minutes in advance.
Spread the flour out on a clean work surface. Add the butter, cut into small pieces.
Form the mixture into a well and add the salt, sugar, egg yolk, and 2 tablespoons of water in the middle.
Mix quickly, taking care not to overwork the dough.
Use the palm of your hand to gently flatten the dough. Shape into a ball and set aside.
For the tart: roll out the dough until it's about 1⁄16 inch (2 mm) thick.
Cut out a 14-inch (35 cm) disc and line a 11-inch (28 cm) buttered tart mold.
Use a fork to prick the base and refrigerate for 15 minutes.
Preheat the oven to 400 °F (200 °C).
Cover the base with parchment paper and fill with dried beans or pie weights.
Bake for 10 to 15 minutes, until lightly golden. Take out of the oven and set aside.

Lemon Cream

Heat the lemon juice, butter, and sugar in a saucepan until the butter has fully melted.
Stir until well combined, then set aside.
In a bowl, beat the eggs until slightly frothy and gradually whisk in the cornstarch.
Slowly pour the lemon mixture into the eggs.
Return the mixture to the saucepan and cook over medium heat, stirring constantly, until it comes to a boil and you obtain a warm, thick mixture.
Transfer to a bowl, cover with plastic wrap pressed onto the surface, and set aside.

Meringue

Beat the egg whites with a pinch of salt.
Slowly add the sugar and beat until the meringue holds firm peaks.
Transfer to a piping bag with the tip of your choice.

Plating

Spoon the lemon cream into the tart shell.
Using a piping bag filled with meringue, cover the surface of the tart, shaping it as desired.
Finally, place the tart under the broiler for a few minutes or gently torch the meringue with a kitchen blowtorch.
Garnish with an edible flower and serve immediately.

m15

· Prawn Tartare and its Hazelnut *Tosta*

· Squid Ink Risotto, Parmesan Foam and Sliced Portobello

· Confit Kid Goat and Potatoes, Glazed Carrot Mirror

· Chocolate *Mille-Feuille*

Chef Elías Murciano

Elías Murciano is a Venezuelan chef and graduate of the Art Institute of Fort Lauderdale, Florida, an institution accredited by the American Culinary Federation (ACF). He has trained under acclaimed chefs including Martín Berasategui, Heinz Winkler, and Alain Ducasse, among others. While in Spain, he opened his second restaurant, Citra, which *The New York Times* hailed as "Madrid's New Favorite Restaurant." He then returned to Venezuela, where he spent six years as head chef at the prestigious Le Gourmet restaurant. He later moved to Panama, where he took the helm as chef and owner of Capital Bistró Panamá. Murciano also serves as partner and director of operations for the Makoto restaurant group in both Latin America and Spain.

Prawn Tartare and its Hazelnut *Tosta*

I fully adapted this recipe to reflect my own style. The original version was a prawn and fish tartare with sweet, Asian flavors, but I opted for a more minimalist approach. My take uses only prawn with a hint of lemon zest, adding a clean, refreshing citrus note. I serve it with a tosta, which is in fact a *tuile au beurre noisette*, with that nutty, almond-like flavor that provides a contrast of textures, resulting in an elegant and very flavorful combination.

4 servings

INGREDIENTS

Tartare
- 7 oz. (200 g) fresh prawns
- 2 tsp. (10 g) lemon zest
- 2 tsp. (10 g) chives
- Olive oil
- Salt
- Black pepper

Hazelnut *Tosta*
- 2 egg whites (60 g)
- 2 tsp. (10 ml) sunflower oil
- 5 tbsp. (70 g) butter
- ⅓ c. + 1 tbsp. (50 g) all-purpose flour
- 1 tbsp. + 1 tsp. (20 g) sugar
- ½ tsp. (2 g) salt

Garnish
- Edible flowers
- Microgreens

PREPARATION

Tartare

Peel and devein the prawns, and cut into fine dice.
Toss with lemon zest, finely minced chives, olive oil, salt, and pepper.
Chill in the refrigerator until ready to use.

Hazelnut *Tosta*

In a small saucepan, melt the butter over medium heat.
Let it cook until golden brown (*beurre noisette*), taking care not to burn it.
Strain the butter through a paper towel to remove the solids.
Chill the butter until firm, then measure out 3 tablespoons (40 g).
Mix the butter with the egg whites, sunflower oil, flour, sugar, and salt until you have a smooth batter.
Spread the batter in a silicone *tuile* mold.
Bake in a preheated oven at 300 °F (150 °C) for 15 minutes.
Cool completely and lift carefully from the mold to prevent cracking.

Plating

Adjust the seasoning of the tartare with olive oil, salt, or pepper if needed.
On a cold plate, mold the tartare in a ring or rectangular shape about ½ inch (1 cm) high.
Gently lift off the mold.
Garnish with edible flowers and microgreens.
Lay the hazelnut *tosta* over the tartare.
Serve immediately.

Squid Ink Risotto, Parmesan Foam and Portobello Slices

This dish brings together intense flavors and creamy textures in a truly indulgent way. The chef swaps rice for pastina in the risotto, creating a pleasantly unexpected result. Arborio or carnaroli rice may also be used following the same procedure, though the cooking time will be longer. I chose to finish the dish with a Parmesan foam rather than an air, adding more body and improving plating stability. Portobello mushrooms lend an earthy, umami depth and a contrasting texture, transforming the risotto into a distinctive and memorable dish.

6 servings

INGREDIENTS

Risotto
- 1 c. (200 g) pastina
- 2 c. (500 ml) squid broth
- ⅓ c. (50 g) onion
- 1 sachet squid ink
- Rum
- Salt
- Black pepper

Portobello
- 1 large portobello mushroom
- Olive oil
- Maldon salt
- Black pepper

Parmesan Foam
- ¾ c. + 1 tbsp. (200 ml) heavy cream
- 1 c. (100 g) grated Parmesan cheese
- ¼ c. + 1 tbsp. (70 ml) whole milk
- 1½ tsp. (8 g) salt

Parsley Oil
- 1 c. (30 g) fresh parsley
- 2 tbsp. (30 ml) olive oil

Garnish
- Edible flower petals
- Microgreens

PREPARATION

Risotto
In a large pot, sauté the onion, finely chopped brunoise-style, in a little butter.
Stir in the pastina, squid ink, and the squid broth.
Add salt and cook, stirring continuously, until the pastina is *al dente*.
Finish with a teaspoon of butter and stir in the Parmesan cheese.

Portobello
Slice the portobello mushroom using a mandoline to 1/16 inch (2 mm) thick.
Arrange the slices on a tray, sprinkle with salt and pepper, and drizzle with olive oil.
Set aside.

Parmesan Foam
Heat the cream, milk, and salt in a saucepan.
As soon as it boils, remove from heat and add the Parmesan.
Stir continuously until the cheese is completely melted.
Transfer to a siphon and insert two charges.
Set aside.

Parsley Oil
Blanch the parsley.
Blend the parsley together with the olive oil until smooth.
Strain the mixture through a fine mesh strainer.

Plating
Just before serving, warm the portobello slices briefly in a nonstick pan, flipping once.
Serve the risotto in a warm dish.
Top with several portobello slices and a few dots of Parmesan foam.
Drizzle with a few drops of parsley oil and garnish with edible flowers and microgreens.
Serve immediately.

Confit Kid Goat with Potatoes, Glazed Carrot Mirror

This dish is a study in refinement, patience, and sensory delight. The confit goat features a crisp, golden exterior that gives way to tender, succulent meat, melting effortlessly with each bite. The potatoes, slow-cooked in the goat's juices, deliver a rich, velvety texture and deep, savory flavor, creating perfect harmony between the meat's richness and the potato's creaminess. Everything rests on a luminous bed of glazed carrot slices, whose gentle sweetness completes the dish with elegant balance.

4 servings

INGREDIENTS

Kid Goat

- 1 leg of kid goat
- ½ head of garlic
- 1 sprig rosemary
- 1 sprig thyme
- 2 c. (500 ml) vegetable oil

Confit Potatoes

- 4 potatoes
- 1½ tbsp. (20 g) butter
- ¾ c. + 1 tbsp. (200 ml) reserved oil from cooking the meat

Kid Goat Jus

- Reserved bones from the kid goat
- 1 c. (150 g) carrot
- ⅓ c. (50 g) onion
- ⅓ c. (50 g) celery
- ¾ c. + 1 tbsp. (200 ml) beef stock
- 3 tbsp. (40 g) butter
- Salt
- Black pepper

Glaze

- ¾ c. + 1 tbsp. (200 ml) kid goat jus
- 2 tbsp. + 2 tsp. (30 g) sugar
- 2 tbsp. (30 g) butter

Glazed Carrots

- 1 lb. 2 oz. (500 g) carrots
- 2 tbsp. (30 g) butter

Garnish

- Microgreens and fresh greens

PREPARATION

Kid Goat

Season the kid goat leg generously with salt and pepper.

Sear in a frying pan with butter until golden on all sides.

Place the leg in a baking tray with garlic, rosemary, and thyme, then submerge fully in oil.

Cook slowly in a static oven at 200 °F (95 °C) until tender.

The cooking time depends on the size of the leg; it may take between 1 and 2 hours or longer.

In this version, the leg cooked for 90 minutes.

Let cool once the meat is cooked through.

Drain the kid goat leg, debone, and divide into individual portions.

Set aside the meat, bones, and the cooking oil.

Confit Potatoes

Peel the potatoes and submerge in cold water.

Dry and shape the potatoes into 1¼-inch (3 cm) cylinders with a round cutter.

If you do not have a round cutter, you can cut the potatoes with a knife, shaping them as you wish to a height of ¾ inch (2 cm).

Place the cylinders in a frying pan and cover with the reserved confit oil.

Cook slowly for about 30 minutes, or until the potatoes are easily pierced with a skewer but do not break apart.

Remove from the heat and set aside.

Kid Goat Jus

Finely dice the carrot, celery and onion.

Sauté in a saucepan with butter.

Once the onion is translucent, add the goat bones.

Add the beef broth and let simmer gently for 20 minutes.

Confit Kid Goat with Potatoes, Glazed Carrot Mirror

Glaze

Strain the kid goat jus through a sieve into a saucepan.

Bring to a boil, then lower the heat.

Add the sugar and let cook for about 5 minutes.

Stir in the butter and combine thoroughly.

Glazed Carrots

Slice the peeled carrots lengthwise into ¹⁄₁₆-inch (2 mm) slices using a mandoline.

In a frying pan, melt the butter and lightly sauté the carrots.

Set aside.

Plating

Just before serving, brush the kid goat with the glaze and place under a hot broiler for a few minutes.

Arrange the carrot slices side by side on a board.

Cut a 2 × 4-inch (5 × 10 cm) rectangle from the carrot layer.

Transfer the carrot base to a hot plate and brush with glaze.

Arrange a portion of kid goat on top of the carrot rectangle.

Add 1 or 2 hot confit potato cylinders.

Garnish with a few microgreens, and serve immediately.

Chocolate *Mille-Feuille*

This dessert is another classic of French pastry, which I decided to include even though it wasn't part of the original menu. Delicate, crisp layers of puff pastry and a smooth, rich chocolate cream take center stage in this *mille-feuille*. For the presentation, I drew inspiration from a dessert I always enjoy at Le Bilboquet in New York, where it's served on its side and features even crispier layers than the traditional version. In this recipe, I managed to double the crunch by sprinkling powdered sugar over the puff pastry before baking, resulting in golden, lightly caramelized layers that pair beautifully with the chocolate mousse, which offers a deep and intense flavor.

6 servings

INGREDIENTS

Pastry Base

- Puff pastry
- Powdered sugar

Chocolate Mousse

- 7 oz. (200 g) dark chocolate
- 3½ tbsp. (50 g) butter
- 2 egg yolks
- 4 egg whites
- ⅔ c. (150 ml) heavy cream
- ¼ c. + 1 tbsp. (60 g) granulated sugar

Garnish

- 1¼ c. (300 ml) heavy cream
- 2 tbsp. (20 g) powdered sugar
- 3½ oz. (100 g) dark couverture chocolate
- Edible flowers

PREPARATION

Pastry Base

Roll out the puff pastry, dusting with powdered sugar as you go until it reaches a thickness of ⅛ inch (3 mm).

Chill in the refrigerator for a few minutes.

Lay the pastry on a silicone mat on a baking sheet, place another mat on top, and gently set another tray on top of the mat to keep it flat.

Bake in a preheated oven at 350 °F (175 °C) for 25 minutes.

Remove when golden, let cool, and cut into 1 × 4-inch (3 × 10 cm) rectangles.

Chocolate Mousse

Use a double boiler to melt the chocolate with the butter.

Add the egg yolks and whisk into the chocolate mixture.

Heat the cream and combine it with the chocolate mixture.

Set aside.

Beat the egg whites to soft peaks, slowly adding the sugar.

Carefully fold the whites into the chocolate base.

Refrigerate for two hours.

Garnish

Whip the heavy cream until stiff peaks form.

Mix in the powdered sugar.

Transfer to a piping bag and set aside.

Melt the chocolate and spread it thinly on an acetate sheet.

Cut into desired shapes using a mold or cutter and let cool.

Carefully detach the chocolate figures and set aside.

Plating

Cover two puff pastry layers with chocolate mousse.

Stack one over the other, then top with a third plain rectangle.

Arrange the *mille-feuille* on its side on the serving plate.

Pipe the whipped cream decoratively over the top, and garnish with chocolate figures and edible flowers.

m16

- *Chipichipi Gelée à la Joël Robuchon*, Masago Parfait, Ocumo Purée, Parsley Gel
- Mini *Asado Negro*
- Arepa Terrine
- Bittersweet Chocolate Truffle Pâté with Sweet Confections

Chef Alonso Núñez

The Venezuelan chef Alonso Nuñez has an extensive career in the culinary arts. A graduate of the Centro de Estudios Gastronómicos (CEGA), his passion for cooking led him to complete internships at renowned international restaurants, including Restaurant Balzac in Paris and Heston Blumenthal's groundbreaking The Fat Duck in the United Kingdom. His experience ranges from classic French haute cuisine to the most cutting-edge techniques of molecular gastronomy. Núñez focuses on highlighting the native flavors of Venezuela, blending them with international influences to create truly unique culinary offerings.

Chipichipi Gelée à la Joël Robuchon, Masago Parfait, Ocumo Purée, Parsley Gel

The original recipe for this dish takes inspiration from *Le Caviar Impérial*, one of the signature creations of French chef Joël Robuchon, though with different ingredients and a slightly reimagined presentation. In my version—somewhat distinct from Núñez's interpretation—I sought to truly evoke Robuchon's refined and meticulous philosophy, where every element contributes texture, flavor, and color, all assembled with precision. The base is a *chipichipi gelée*, delivering a pure, oceanic essence. Resting atop it is a silky masago parfait, whose delicate sweetness and subtle bursts of seafood flavor create a unique textural experience. These flavors find balance in the ocumo (or malanga) purée, which offers an earthy, faintly sweet note. Finally, a parsley gel adds both a visual accent and aromatic lift, bringing the dish into perfect harmony.

4 servings

INGREDIENTS

Chipichipi Stock

- 4 lb. 6 oz. (2 kg) *chipichipi* or other shellfish
- 2 lb. 3 oz. (1 kg) white fish heads
- 1½ c. (200 g) leek
- 1½ c. (200 g) carrot
- 1 head of garlic
- 4¼ c. (1.25 l) water

Chipichipi Gelée

- 2 c. (500 ml) *chipichipi* stock
- ½ sheet (3 g) sheet gelatin

Parfait

- ⅓ c. (80 ml) heavy cream
- 4 egg yolks (80 g)
- 3 tbsp. (45 g) masago
- 3½ tbsp. (50 g) butter
- 2 tbsp. (30 ml) *chipichipi* stock
- 1 tbsp. (15 ml) white wine
- 2 large egg whites, beaten to stiff peaks
- ½ sheet (1 g) sheet gelatin

Ocumo Purée

- 1¾ c. (450 ml) *chipichipi* stock
- 4 c. (500 g) *ocumo chino* (Chinese taro)
- 1½ tbsp. (20 g) butter
- 3½ tbsp. (50 ml) heavy cream
- Salt
- White pepper

Parsley Extract

- 1 oz. (30 g) curly parsley
- 2 tbsp. + 2 tsp. (40 ml) chicken or vegetable stock
- Salt

Parsley Gel

- ¾ c. + 1 tbsp. (200 g) parsley extract (see below)
- 1 tsp. (2.5 g) agar-agar
- Salt

PREPARATION

Chipichipi Stock

Rinse the *chipichipi* shells well to remove any sand or debris.

Combine all ingredients in a pot and simmer over medium heat for 1 hour.

Strain and allow the liquid to rest for 1 hour.

Filter once more using a moistened cheesecloth to catch any residual grit, being careful not to disturb the sediment at the bottom.

Adjust seasoning; keep warm and set aside.

Chipichipi Gelée

Bloom the gelatin sheets in a small amount of water, squeeze out excess liquid, and gently melt in the microwave for a few seconds without boiling.

Stir the melted gelatin into the *chipichipi* stock.

Blend until fully combined and chill.

When it starts to gel, spoon into the shallow bowls where it will be plated.

Cover each bowl and refrigerate.

Parfait

Beat the egg yolks until they turn pale and airy.

Gently heat the heavy cream, without letting it boil.

Pour a small amount of hot cream into the yolks to temper them.

Add the rest of the cream and stir until smooth.

Chipichipi Gelée à la Joël Robuchon, Masago Parfait, Ocumo Purée, Parsley Gel

Stir in the melted butter.
Add the stock and white wine, mixing until the texture is smooth and uniform.
Bloom the gelatin sheets in a small amount of water.
Remove excess liquid, and gently melt in the microwave for a few seconds without boiling.
Add the melted gelatin into the prepared mixture.
Carefully fold in the egg whites, previously beaten to stiff peaks.
Stir in one tablespoon of masago.
Arrange four 1½-inch (4 cm) pastry rings on a tray.
Spoon the parfait mixture into the rings, leaving a 2 mm gap at the top.
Cover with plastic wrap and chill until the parfaits are firm

Ocumo Purée
Peel the ocumo and cut into round slices.
Boil until tender.
Process in a blender until you obtain a smooth purée.
Melt the butter in a small pan over low heat.
Stir in the ocumo and gradually add the hot stock while mixing.
Bring to a boil.
Drain, season, and refrigerate.
Just before plating, reheat the purée and mix in some heavy cream to achieve the perfect purée texture.
Transfer to a piping bag and set aside.

Parsley Extract
Rinse and trim the parsley, and remove the stems.
Blanch the parsley in salted water and immediately transfer it to an ice bath.
Blend the parsley with the stock just until a smooth mixture forms.
Adjust salt to taste.

Parsley Gel
Measure out ¾ cup plus 1 tablespoon (200 g) of parsley extract and pour into a small pan.
Add the agar-agar and bring to a boil, stirring constantly.
Remove from heat and pour into a tray.
Place plastic wrap directly on the surface to prevent a skin from forming.
Chill for about 2 hours until set.
Remove from tray and blend into a smooth gel.
Strain through a fine mesh sieve.
Transfer to a squeeze bottle and set aside.

Plating
Take the plated *chipichipi gelée* out of the refrigerator.
With the help of a spatula, place the ring with the parfait mixture in the center of the bowl.
Spread a thin layer of Capelin roe over the parfait to fully cover the surface.
Pipe dots of purée around the ring, working from the inside out.
Add smaller dots of parsley gel over the purée dots.
Carefully lift off the ring and serve immediately.

Mini *Asado Negro*

Asado negro is a classic dish from Venezuela, and I was pleased to feature it on this menu. Although I've made a few slight adjustments, it still preserves its discreetly sweet flavor and the signature dark color that give it its name. To give the sauce more depth, I used a high-quality French red wine. I paired it with an arepa terrine to complete the dish's Venezuelan character.

4 servings

INGREDIENTS

Marinade
- 3 lb. 5 oz. (1.5 kg) eye of round
- 1½ c. (200 g) scallions
- 1½ c. (200 g) onion
- 1½ c. (200 g) red bell pepper
- 1½ c. (200 g) *ají dulce* (sweet chili pepper)
- 1½ c. (200 g) leek
- ⅔ c. (150 ml) Worcestershire sauce
- 1 tbsp. (15 ml) orange juice
- 2 tsp. (10 g) garlic paste
- Freshly ground black pepper

Asado Negro
- ¼ c. (60 ml) corn oil
- 1½ tbsp. (20 g) butter
- 2 tbsp. (30 g) grated panela
- 4¼ c. (1 l) water
- ⅓ c. + 1 tbsp. (100 ml) red wine

Garnish
- Microgreens

PREPARATION

Marinade

The day before preparing the dish, cut the meat into rectangular pieces weighing about 9 ounces (250 g) each.

Rub the meat with freshly ground pepper and garlic paste.

Slice the scallions, onions, red bell pepper, *ají dulce*, and leek into fine julienne strips.

Add the sliced vegetables to the marinade.

Add the Worcestershire sauce, corn oil, and orange juice.

Combine thoroughly and cover. Marinate in the refrigerator overnight.

Remove the meat from the marinade and blot dry with paper towels.

Skewer each piece of meat lengthwise with a wooden stick. Set aside.

Asado Negro

In a large pot, heat the oil over high heat and add the butter and grated panela.

Once it begins to caramelize, add the meat and sear, turning to brown evenly.

Remove the meat and set aside.

Add the drained marinade to the same pot.

Sauté until it reduces and browns.

Add the water and reserved meat.

Cover and simmer over low heat for around 3 hours, turning the meat often.

Allow the meat to cool in its braising liquid for about 4 hours.

Remove the meat from the pot.

Strain the sauce, pressing the solids against the sides of the sieve.

Remove any excess fat from the surface.

Return the strained liquid and the meat to the pot.

Add the red wine and simmer over medium heat for about 20 minutes, allowing the sauce to reduce slightly. Let rest for at least 1 hour.

Plating

Remove the skewers from each piece of meat and cut each mini *asado* into two portions.

Place two or three pieces of meat on a warm plate.

Spoon the sauce over the meat.

Accompany with a piece of arepa terrine.

Garnish with fresh herbs or microgreens.

Serve immediately.

Arepa Terrine

The arepa is a traditional Venezuelan food, but in this case the chef transforms it into a terrine, the French term for molded preparations where ingredients are layered, pressed, and baked into a cohesive form. The result is an unexpected delight: the taste of corn merges beautifully with the soft, creamy character of fresh white cheese—both distinctly Latin American flavors.

4 servings

INGREDIENTS

Terrine

- 13 oz. (375 g) day-old arepas, cold
- ¾ c. (180 ml) whole milk
- 8¾ oz. (250 g) *queso de mano* (a traditional Venezuelan fresh cheese)
- ¾ c. (75 g) grated Parmesan cheese
- ¾ c. (80 g) grated hard white cheese, not too salty

Bechamel

- 2 tbsp. (30 g) butter
- ⅓ c. (80 ml) whole milk
- ⅓ c. (40 g) all-purpose flour
- ½ tsp. salt
- 1½ tbsp. butter
- Butter, for greasing the pan

PREPARATION

About 2 hours before making the gratin, split the arepas and place them in the milk to soak.

Bechamel

Heat the butter in a saucepan and add the flour, stirring well.
Pour in the rest of the milk, including the milk used to soak the arepas.
Season with salt.
Let cook for around 10 minutes, or until the mixture thickens.
Set aside.

Terrine

Preheat the oven to 400 °F (200 °C).
Grease a rectangular terrine mold with butter.
Combine the grated cheeses in a bowl.
Fill the mold with alternating layers of sauce, arepas, and cheese.
Top with a final layer of shredded *queso de mano* and small pieces of butter.
Bake uncovered for about 35 minutes, or until golden.
Allow to cool slightly, then unmold and slice.

Bittersweet Chocolate Truffle Pâté with Sweet Confections

This menu had to end with chocolate, another fundamental ingredient of Venezuelan identity. That is why I chose this pâté, a luscious and distinctive dessert. I only modified the filling, using marshmallows and fruit gummies instead of *granjerías*, because they are more accessible and just as flavorful. The result is a chocolate block with a creamy center, somewhere between a fondant and a truffle. Every bite balances the richness of chocolate, the airy texture of marshmallow, and the fruity chew of candied guava. It is a genuine symphony of textures and contrasts in every bite.

6 servings

INGREDIENTS

Chocolate Pâté

- 14 oz. (400 g) bittersweet chocolate
- ¾ c. (180 g) unsalted butter
- ¼ c. (60 ml) whole milk
- 4 egg yolks (80 g)
- 1¼ c. (30 g) marshmallows
- 2 tbsp. (30 g) guava *pâte de fruit*
- 2 tbsp. (30 g) fruit gummies

Crème Anglaise

- 4 egg yolks (80 g)
- ¼ c. + 1 tbsp. (60 g) sugar
- 1 c. (240 ml) whole milk
- 1 tsp. vanilla extract

Garnish

- Edible flowers

PREPARATION

Chocolate Pâté

Line the inside of a tall, rectangular mold with parchment paper.
Scrape off any sugar from the guava *pâté de fruit* and fruit gummies, rinsing briefly if necessary.
Slice into sticks, not too thin, bearing in mind that they should be visible when the terrine is sliced.
Set up a double boiler using a heatproof glass or metal bowl.
Place the roughly chopped chocolate in the bowl.
Melt over medium heat.
Add the butter and let it melt, stirring with a spatula to emulsify.
In a separate bowl, whisk the milk and egg yolks together until smooth.
Strain the mixture and add it to the chocolate.
Stir continuously for 5 minutes.
Remove from heat and allow the mixture to settle.
The mixture should be completely emulsified, with no separation between fat and chocolate.
Pour a portion of the chocolate into the prepared mold.
Arrange the marshmallows, fruit gummies, and *pâté de fruit* lengthwise on top of the chocolate.
Cover with more chocolate.
Refrigerate until partially set, but not firm.
Add the remaining marshmallows, fruit gummies, and *pâté de fruit*.
Pour in the remaining chocolate to cover.
Cover and chill until fully set.

Crème Anglaise

Heat the milk with the vanilla until just below boiling.
In a separate bowl, whisk the egg yolks with the sugar until light and pale.
Gradually add the hot milk while continuing to whisk.
Continue to heat while stirring constantly.
Cook until the mixture thickens slightly or coats the back of a spoon.
The ideal temperature is between 180–183 °F (82–84 °C).
Remove from heat as soon as it thickens and strain into a bowl through a fine sieve.
Let cool to room temperature.
Chill until ready to serve.

Bittersweet Chocolate Truffle Pâté with Sweet Confections

Plating

Remove the pâté from the refrigerator 1 hour before serving.

Unmold onto a cutting board.

Remove the parchment paper.

Rinse a long, sharp knife with hot water and use it to slice the pâté without pressing down too hard.

Arrange 2 or 3 slices of chocolate pâté on each plate.

Garnish with edible flowers.

Serve with the *crème anglaise* on the side.

m17

- Carrot Cream, Blue Cheese and Glazed Carrots
- Mediterranean Tartare, Pita Chips
- *Magret de Canard, Sauce Rhum Orange*, Duo of Purées, and Balsamic Reduction
- Passion Fruit Mousse, Blackberry Coulis and Almond *Tuile*

Chef David Posner

Trained at the Culinary Institute of America, the Venezuelan chef David Posner interned at prestigious establishments including Daniel by Daniel Boulud and El Racó de Can Fabes by Santi Santamaria. He launched his career in Venezuela at the landmark Restaurante Ara, and then became both chef and founding partner of Ara Café. He later held the role of Food and Beverage Director at Marriott Dadeland in Miami, and since 2019 has served as Director of Operations at Levy Restaurants.

Carrot Cream, Blue Cheese and Glazed Carrots

This soup is ideal for fans of creamy vegetable soups. I modified the original formula to achieve a purer carrot taste, for a cream that is naturally sweet, silky in texture, and bright in color. The blue cheese adds a layer of complexity, bringing salty notes and a creamy touch that contrasts beautifully with the sweetness of this tuber. The glazed carrots contribute a subtle brilliance and a deep flavor, enriching the experience and creating a perfect balance between sweet and savory.

4-6 servings

INGREDIENTS

Carrot Cream

· 2 lb. 3 oz. (1 kg) carrots
· ⅓ c. (50 g) onion
· 4¼ c. (1 l) chicken stock
· 2 tbsp. (30 g) butter

Blue Cheese Cream

· 2 tbsp. (30 ml) chicken stock
· 1¾ oz. (50 g) blue cheese
· ¾ c. + 1 tbsp. (100 ml) heavy cream

Glazed Carrots

· 1⅓ c. (200 g) carrots
· 3½ tbsp. (50 ml) chicken stock
· 3½ tbsp. (50 ml) honey
· 3½ tbsp. (50 g) butter

Tuile

· 3½ tbsp. (50 g) butter
· ⅓ c. + 1 tbsp. (50 g) all-purpose flour
· 1½ egg whites (50 g)
· 1 tsp. (5 g) salt

Garnish

· Microgreens

PREPARATION

Carrot Cream

Roughly chop the carrots and onion.
Sauté in a saucepan with butter.
Add the chicken stock and cook for about 30 minutes, until the carrots are tender.
Blend on high speed for 2 to 3 minutes until smooth and creamy.
Strain the mixture and return it to the saucepan.

Blue Cheese Cream

Heat the chicken stock with the blue cheese until fully melted.
Allow to cool.
Whip the heavy cream until it doubles in volume and fold in the blue cheese.
Transfer to a squeeze bottle and set aside.

Glazed Carrots

Chop the carrots into very small dice.
Sauté in butter, taking care they don't brown.
Add the chicken stock and honey, and cook until the carrots are tender and the liquid has evaporated.
Set aside.

Tuile

Combine all ingredients.
Spread the mixture onto a *tuile* mold into the desired shape.
Bake in a preheated oven at 350 °F (175 °C) for 5 minutes.

Plating

Ladle the hot carrot cream into a warm bowl.
Garnish with dots of blue cheese cream, a *tuile*, and small bits of glazed carrot.
Garnish with a few microgreens, and serve immediately.

Mediterranean Tartare, Pita Chips

This starter brings together fresh, light Mediterranean textures and flavors. The tartare is made with sea bass and paired with a quinoa tabbouleh instead of bulgur, offering a more modern and health-conscious version. The golden, crunchy pita chips provide a perfect contrast to the softness of the tartare and tabbouleh, resulting in an appetizer that is both vibrant and delicious.

4-6 servings

INGREDIENTS

Tartare
- 1 lb. 5 oz. (600 g) sea bass
- 1 c. (120 g) red onion
- ⅓ c. (80 ml) extra virgin olive oil
- Salt
- Black pepper

Quinoa Tabbouleh
- 3½ oz. (100 g) parsley
- 1 c. (200 g) quinoa
- 1¾ c. (400 ml) water
- 1 c. (125 g) red onion
- ⅓ c. + 1 tbsp. (100 ml) olive oil
- ⅓ c. + 1 tbsp. (100 ml) lemon juice
- Salt
- Black pepper

Chips
- 3 rounds of pita bread
- Olive oil
- Salt

Garnish
- Microgreens

PREPARATION

Tartare

Dice the sea bass into very small cubes and the red onion into a fine brunoise.

In a bowl, mix the fish, onion, and olive oil.

Season with salt and pepper.

Refrigerate to marinate until ready to serve.

Quinoa Tabbouleh

Cook the quinoa in lightly salted boiling water for several minutes, until all the water is absorbed, then set aside.

Dice the red onion into a fine brunoise.

Finely chop the parsley.

In a bowl, combine the quinoa with the onion, parsley, olive oil, and lemon juice.

Season with salt and pepper to taste.

Set aside.

Chips

Split the pita bread into 2 thinner layers.

Cut into small wedges and bake with olive oil and salt until golden and crisp.

Plating

Center a ring mold or mold of your choice on a plate.

Spoon in a layer of quinoa tabbouleh into the mold.

Top with a layer of sea bass tartare.

Garnish with microgreens.

Serve with the pita chips on the side.

Magret de Canard, Sauce Rhum Orange, Duo of Purées, and Balsamic Reduction

This dish strikes a balance between refinement and simplicity. The duck magret is tender and juicy, with golden-crisp skin that amplifies its deep flavor. The rum-orange sauce is thick and aromatic, adding caramelized and citrus notes along with an attractive gloss. The mashed potatoes provide a creamy counterpoint to the richness of the meat, while the carrot purée adds a touch of sweetness and visual brightness with its light, smooth texture. Finally, the balsamic reduction contributes an extra layer of acidic, subtly sweet flavor that elevates the magret even further.

4 servings

INGREDIENTS

Magret de Canard
- 4 duck breasts
- Salt
- Black pepper

Sauce Rhum Orange
- 1½ c. (350 ml) dark duck stock
- 1½ c. (200 g) onion
- 3½ tbsp. (50 g) garlic
- 1 c. (150 g) celery
- ⅓ c. (40 g) all-purpose flour
- 1 orange
- ⅓ c. + 1 tbsp. (100 ml) honey
- 1 c. (250 ml) orange juice
- ⅔ c. (150 ml) rum
- 3½ tbsp. (50 g) butter

Carrot Purée
- 2 c. (300 g) carrots
- ⅓ c. + 1 tbsp. (100 ml) chicken stock

Potato Purée
- 1 lb. 2 oz. (500 g) potatoes
- 1 c. (250 ml) whole milk
- ½ c. + 1 tbsp. (125 g) butter
- 1 tsp. (5 g) salt

Balsamic Reduction
- 1 c. (250 ml) balsamic vinegar
- 1 tbsp. + 1 tsp. (20 g) sugar

Garnish
- Microgreens

PREPARATION

Magret de Canard

Lay the cleaned and dried duck breasts on a cutting board.
Place in the freezer for a few minutes until the skin firms up slightly.
Score the skin side delicately in a diagonal pattern without cutting into the meat.
Season with salt and pepper.
Cook skin-side down in a frying pan over moderate heat, without adding any fat.
Occasionally remove excess rendered fat.
Cook for 6 to 7 minutes, or until the skin is lightly golden.
Flip and sear the other side for 1 to 2 minutes.
Transfer to a baking tray and set aside.

Sauce Rhum Orange

Coarsely chop the onion, garlic, and celery.
Sauté the vegetables in butter.
Add the flour and cook a bit longer.
Add the rum and bring to a boil.
Stir in the orange juice and honey.
Let the sauce reduce by half.
Add the dark duck stock and 2 or 3 strips of orange peel.
Reduce until the desired consistency is reached.
Adjust salt to taste.
Set aside.

Carrot Purée

Slice the carrots into rounds and add to a saucepan.
Cover with the chicken stock.
Simmer gently until the carrots are tender.

Magret de Canard, Sauce Rhum Orange, Duo of Purées, and Balsamic Reduction

Drain and purée at high speed for 2 minutes with as little liquid as possible until silky and glossy.
Add the butter and blend again until smooth.
Season with salt, transfer to a squeeze bottle, and set aside.

Potato Purée
Wash the potatoes well and add them to a pot.
Cover with water and bring to a boil.
Once cooked, peel the potatoes and press them through a potato ricer.
Return the puréed potatoes to the pot and reheat, stirring constantly with a spatula.
Add the cold butter cut into small cubes.
Continue stirring and gradually add hot milk until you obtain the desired consistency.
Adjust salt to taste, transfer to a piping bag, and set aside.

Balsamic Reduction
Combine the vinegar and sugar in a saucepan.
Simmer over medium heat for about 20 minutes, or until it reaches a syrup-like consistency.
Remove from heat and set aside.

Plating
Preheat the oven to 380 °F (190 °C).
Place the duck breasts in the oven for 4–5 minutes, or until the internal temperature reaches about 130 °F (55 °C).
Let rest for 5–8 minutes; the temperature will rise to about 135 °F (57 °C) for a medium-rare finish.
Slice the magret diagonally into pieces about ¼ inch (6–7 mm) thick.
Arrange the duck slices on a preheated plate.
Pipe a line of mashed potatoes alongside the duck.
Dot the plate with carrot purée and balsamic reduction.
Spoon over the warm orange sauce, garnish with microgreens, and serve immediately.

Passion Fruit Mousse, Blackberry Coulis and Almond *Tuile*

This dessert makes a strong visual impression with its vibrant contrast of colors. It features a silky passion fruit mousse with a refreshing tropical flavor, paired with a blackberry coulis that offers a sweet-and-tart contrast and a touch of vibrant purple. The fine and crunchy *tuile* adds an interesting texture and nutty flavor that perfectly complements the dish, creating an exquisite experience of flavors, colors, and textures.

4-6 servings

INGREDIENTS

Passion Fruit Mousse

- ¾ c. + 1 tbsp. (200 ml) passion fruit concentrate
- ⅔ c. + 1 tbsp. (140 g) sugar
- 0.21 oz. (6 g) gelatin
- ¾ c. + 1 tbsp. (200 ml) heavy cream
- 2½ egg whites (70 g)

Blackberry-Balsamic Coulis

- 1 c. (150 g) blackberries
- ⅓ c. (75 g) sugar
- 3½ tbsp. (50 ml) balsamic vinegar
- 3½ tbsp. (50 ml) water

Almond *Tuile*

- 1½ egg whites (50 g)
- ¼ c. (50 g) sugar
- ⅓ c. + 1 tbsp. (50 g) all-purpose flour
- 3½ tbsp. (50 g) butter
- 1 c. (100 g) sliced almonds

Garnish

- Edible flowers

PREPARATION

Mousse

Heat the passion fruit concentrate and pulse twice in a high-speed blender.
Strain into a bowl and set aside.
Bloom the gelatin in cold water.
Microwave for 5 seconds to dissolve and mix into the passion fruit juice.
Whip the heavy cream to soft peaks.
Gently fold the whipped cream into the passion fruit concentrate.
Beat the egg whites, gradually adding the sugar until soft peaks form.
Fold the meringue into the passion fruit and cream mixture.
Pour into molds (preferably flexible) where the mousse will be prepared.
Refrigerate for at least 2–3 hours.

Blackberry Coulis

Bring the blackberries and the water to a boil in a small saucepan.
Strain through a fine sieve to extract all the pulp.
Return the pulp to the pan and heat with the sugar and balsamic vinegar.
Simmer over low heat until it reaches a syrup-like consistency.

Almond *Tuile*

Combine all ingredients except the sliced almonds.
Spread thin circles of the mixture onto a baking sheet lined with a silicone mat.
Sprinkle the sliced almonds on top of each circle.
Bake at 350 °F (175 °C) for 5 to 7 minutes.
While still soft, shape as desired and let cool.

Plating

Place the mousse molds in the freezer for a few minutes to firm up for easier handling.
Spoon a little blackberry coulis into a shallow bowl.
Unmold the mousse and place it on top of the coulis.
Top with 1 or 2 almond *tuiles* and garnish with edible flowers.
Serve immediately.

m18

· Salmon Gravlax

· Three-Mushroom Gnocchi

· Lamb Gigot with Potatoes in Two Textures

· Chocolate Mousse, Orange *Tuile*

Chef David Posner

Trained at the Culinary Institute of America, the Venezuelan chef David Posner interned at prestigious establishments including Daniel by Daniel Boulud and El Racó de Can Fabes by Santi Santamaria. He launched his career in Venezuela at the landmark Restaurante Ara, and then became both chef and founding partner of Ara Café. He later held the role of Food and Beverage Director at Marriott Dadeland in Miami, and since 2019 has served as Director of Operations at Levy Restaurants.

Salmon Gravlax

This is a modern variation on classic gravlax, which is usually marinated for 24 hours or more under weight to press out moisture. In this case, the marinating time is shorter, and no weight is used. This approach highlights the fresh, natural taste of the salmon, preserves more moisture, and yields a tender fish with a smooth, silky texture that cuts like butter. The sour cream sauce adds gentle acidity and replaces the traditional mustard sauce with a lighter touch.

6 servings

INGREDIENTS

Salmon Gravlax
- 2 lb. 3 oz. (1 kg) salmon fillet
- ½ c. + 2 tbsp. (120 g) sugar
- ½ c. + 2 tbsp. (120 g) salt
- 1 tbsp. (15 g) ground black pepper
- 2 tsp. (10 ml) vodka

Sauce
- ⅓ c. (80 g) sour cream
- 1½ tbsp. (24 ml) lemon juice
- Salt
- Black pepper

Garnish
- Dill sprig
- Micro arugula
- Chives

PREPARATION

Salmon Gravlax

Marinate the salmon in salt, sugar, vodka, and black pepper.

Refrigerate for 12 hours.

Rinse the salmon lightly with water to clean off the cure.

Lay on a clean cloth to dry well.

Chill until ready to use.

Sauce

Mix all the ingredients and transfer to a squeeze bottle.

Plating

Cut the salmon into ⅙-inch (4 mm) slices.

Arrange 3 slices on a plate.

Garnish with small dots of sauce and sprigs of dill, micro arugula, and chives.

Three-Mushroom Gnocchi

Gnocchi, a classic of Italian cuisine with a soft, tender texture, are usually made with potatoes, though other ingredients can also be used. In this version, they're served with a sauce made from three types of mushrooms, offering a deep, earthy aroma that infuses the dish and a creamy texture that ties all the elements together. What sets this recipe apart is the plating, where I gave the dish a modern touch by placing each gnocchi individually on the plate, turning every bite into a burst of flavor.

6 servings

INGREDIENTS

Gnocchi

- 2 lb. 3 oz. (1 kg) potatoes
- 2 c. + 1 tbsp. (250 g) all-purpose flour
- 1 tbsp. + 1 tsp. (20 g) salt
- 3 eggs (150 g)

Sauce

- 3½ c. (500 g) white button mushrooms
- 3½ c. (500 g) oyster mushrooms
- 1½ c. (200 g) shiitake mushrooms
- 7 tbsp. (100 g) minced garlic
- ⅔ c. (150 ml) white wine
- 1¼ c. (300 ml) chicken stock
- 1 c. (250 ml) heavy cream
- 4 tbsp. (60 ml) truffle oil
- 1¾ oz. (50 g) chopped parsley

Garnish

- Microgreens

PREPARATION

Gnocchi

Sprinkle the potatoes with salt and bake with the skin on for 1 hour.
Peel and press through a potato ricer or food mill.
Mix the purée with the flour and the eggs.
Transfer the dough to a piping bag and pipe into ⅝-inch (1.5 cm) pieces.
Press each gnocchi gently with the back of a fork to make ridges.
Arrange on a tray dusted with flour.
Set aside.

Sauce

Sauté the 3 types of mushrooms in olive oil until lightly caramelized, then add the minced garlic.
Add the white wine and reduce by half.
Stir in the chicken stock and allow to reduce slightly.
Finish with the heavy cream and cook until the desired consistency is reached.

Plating

Boil the gnocchi in salted water until they float.
Sauté in butter until lightly golden.
Spoon the sauce onto a preheated plate and arrange the gnocchi on top.
Finish with chopped parsley and a few drops of truffle oil.
Garnish with a few microgreens and serve immediately.

Lamb Gigot with Potatoes in Two Textures

This lamb gigot dish is not the original recipe, but one of my longtime staples that had to be included in this book. The tender, juicy meat with its deep, complex flavor is perfectly complemented by the glossy sauce, which brings together the richness of the lamb and the robust character of the wine. I served it with potatoes prepared in two textures, creating a contrast between the creaminess of the purée and the crispness of the potato slice. This contrast elevates the whole experience, making each bite balanced and memorable.

4-6 servings

INGREDIENTS

Lamb Gigot
· 1 leg of lamb
· 5½ c. (800 g) onion
· 1¼ c. (300 ml) red wine
· ¾ oz. (20 g) fresh thyme
· 3½ tbsp. (50 ml) olive oil

Sauce
· Cooking juices
· ½ c. + 1 tbsp. (50 g) butter

Potato Purée
· 1 lb. 2 oz. (500 g) potatoes
· 1 c. (250 ml) whole milk
· ½ c. + 1 tbsp. (125 g) butter
· 1 tsp. (5 g) salt

Crispy Potato Slices
· 9 oz. (250 g) potatoes
· ¼ c. (30 g) cornstarch
· Neutral oil

PREPARATION

Lamb Gigot
Trim the leg of lamb and season with salt and pepper.
Heat the olive oil in a pot large enough to hold the leg of lamb.
Sear the meat over high heat until golden on all sides.
Transfer to a plate and set aside.
Slice the onion into julienne and add to the same pot.
Sauté until soft and golden.
Add a few sprigs of thyme, and season with salt and pepper.
Transfer the onions to a deep roasting pan.
Add the lamb and the red wine.
Cover well with aluminum foil to seal.
Roast at 320 °F (160 °C) for about 3 hours, or until the meat is very tender.
Once done, transfer the lamb to a cutting board for portioning.

Sauce
Once the meat is removed, strain the pan juices.
Transfer the liquid to a saucepan and simmer for a few minutes.
Add the cold butter in pieces and whisk vigorously to emulsify.
Reduce until the desired consistency is reached.
Set aside.

Potato Purée
Wash the potatoes thoroughly and place in a pot.
Cover with water and bring to a boil.
Once cooked, peel the potatoes and press them through a potato ricer or food mill.
Transfer the puréed potatoes to a pot and reheat, stirring constantly with a spatula.
Add the cold butter cut into small cubes.
Continue stirring and gradually add hot milk until you obtain a creamy purée.
Season with salt to taste and set aside.

Crispy Potato Slices
Boil the potatoes with a pinch of salt until tender.
Dissolve the cornstarch in a teaspoon of water.
Blend the cooked potatoes together with the cornstarch mixture.

Lamb Gigot with Potatoes in Two Textures

Add some oil while blending to achieve a smooth, creamy consistency.

Spread the mixture evenly with a spatula on a silicone mat to about 1 mm thick.

Bake at 220 °F (105 °C) for 1 hour, or until dry and crisp.

Break or cut into pieces and fry in hot oil until golden.

Drain on paper towels and set aside.

Plating

Reheat the lamb in the sauce.

On a preheated plate, place a portion of lamb, some dots of mashed potato, and a piece of the crispy potato slice on top.

Accompany with more sauce, garnish, and serve immediately.

Chocolate Mousse, Orange *Tuile*

The original version of this recipe yielded a slightly heavier mousse. In this version, however, I achieved a lighter texture by adjusting a few of the ingredients. The result is a smooth and creamy mousse with a delicate chocolate flavor. It is without a doubt an easy, delicious recipe that never fails.

If you don't have a silicone mold to shape the mousse, you can simply place it in a container and let it chill just the same. Serve using an ice cream scoop, or form a quenelle.

4-6 servings

INGREDIENTS

Chocolate Mousse

- 6¼ oz. (175 g) dark chocolate (70% cocoa)
- ⅓ c. + 1 tbsp. (100 ml) heavy cream
- 2 tbsp. (30 g) butter
- 2 tbsp. (30 ml) whole milk
- 2 egg yolks, at room temperature
- 5 egg whites
- 3 tbsp. + 1 tsp. (40 g) sugar
- 2 tsp. (6 g) gelatin

Orange *Tuile*

- 2 egg whites (50 g)
- 1 orange (juice and zest)
- ¾ c. (90 g) powdered sugar
- ⅔ c. (80 g) all-purpose flour
- 3½ tbsp. (50 g) melted butter

Garnish

- Edible flowers
- 3½ oz. (100 g) couverture chocolate (optional)

PREPARATION

Chocolate Mousse

Bring the milk and cream to a boil.

Bloom the gelatin, then add to the milk and cream mixture.

Pour this mixture over the chocolate and butter and melt gently over a double boiler.

Add the lightly beaten egg yolks with half of the sugar.

In a separate bowl, beat the egg whites to stiff peaks with the remaining sugar.

Gently fold the egg whites into the chocolate mixture.

Pour the mixture into silicone molds of the desired shape and freeze for 4 hours.

Orange *Tuile*

Combine all ingredients until smooth.

Place a tablespoon of the mixture on a *tuile* mold or silicone baking mat and spread it thinly with a spatula.

Bake at 350 °F (175 °C) for 5 to 7 minutes, or until the edges begin to brown.

Remove from the oven and carefully lift the *tuiles* off the tray.

Let cool and set.

Chocolate Garnish

Chop the chocolate into small bits.

Transfer to a bowl and melt over a double boiler.

Spread a thin 1 mm layer of chocolate onto an acetate sheet.

When it begins to crystallize but before it hardens, cut into 4 × 0.8-inch (3 × 2 cm) rectangles.

Drape over a rolling pin and let dry.

Set aside.

Plating

Unmold the mousse and place it on a plate.

Place an orange *tuile* on top of the mousse.

You can also make figures from couverture chocolate and place them on top.

Garnish and serve immediately.

m19

· Foie Gras, Brioche, *Gelée* and Mango Chutney

· Herb and Pistachio-Crusted *Carré d'Agneau*, Semolina and Ratatouille

· Chocolate Gratin with Caramelized Pineapple, Praline Cylinder

Chef Jean-Marc Réal

Celebrated for his creativity and understated talent, the French chef Jean-Marc Réal leads the kitchen at his restaurant, Le Saint Martial, located in the village of Saint-Martial de Nabirat. The restaurant features a charming contemporary atmosphere and two small dining rooms warmly and humorously hosted by his wife, Valérie, who recommends wines and describes the dishes. Each dish reflects a deep respect for the ingredients. His cooking is marked by a variety of flavors, cooking techniques, and complementary textures. The couple also prioritizes local ingredients, sourcing them directly from well-known producers throughout France. Jean-Marc Réal brings years of experience in the kitchens of various Relais & Châteaux establishments such as Le Vieux Logis and Château du Breuil, among others.

Foie Gras, Brioche, *Gelée* and Mango Chutney

Although I adapted this recipe almost completely, the preparation of the foie gras remains simple and exquisite. What I changed was the pairing: in the original version, it was served with marinated vegetable *tagliatelle*. For the plating, I drew inspiration from French chef Tristan Cabirol, originally from the Bordeaux region, who presents his dishes with elegance and finesse. This dish is built from small squares of brioche, *gelée*, and mango chutney, resulting in a sophisticated, balanced combination that delights with every bite.

4 servings

INGREDIENTS

Foie Gras

- 1 raw foie gras (about 1½ lb. / 700 g)
- 4¼ c. (1 kg) coarse salt
- 1¼ c. (250 g) muscovado sugar
- 1 tbsp. black pepper

Mango *Gelée*

- ⅔ c. (150 g) mango purée
- 3 sheets gelatin
- 4 tbsp. orange juice
- 2 tbsp. sugar

Mango Chutney

- 3½ tbsp. (1¾ oz. / 50 g) mango
- ⅓ c. + 1 tbsp. (100 ml) rice vinegar
- ⅓ c. + 1 tbsp. (90 g) sugar
- 3½ tbsp. (1¾ oz. / 50 g) orange juice

Brioche

- 4 slices of brioche
- Butter

Balsamic Caramel

- 1¼ c. (300 ml) balsamic vinegar

Garnish

- Green apple
- Microgreens
- Edible flowers

PREPARATION

Foie Gras

Separate the 2 lobes of the foie gras and carefully remove the veins using a paring knife.

Lay a piece of cheesecloth flat on a work surface and place the foie gras on top.

Wrap it in the cheesecloth to form a roll.

Twist both ends of the cloth to compress the foie gras into a compact cylinder, like a sausage.

Combine the coarse salt, muscovado sugar, and pepper in a glass baking dish.

Submerge the foie gras completely in the curing mixture.

Chill for at least 21 hours.

Remove the foie gras from the salt mixture and store in the fridge.

Mango *Gelée*

Heat the orange juice with the sugar until fully dissolved.

Blend the mango pulp until smooth and uniform.

Press the mango through a strainer to remove the fibers and then add to the orange juice.

Mix well to combine.

Bloom the gelatin in cold water.

Remove excess liquid and heat in the microwave for 10 seconds to dissolve.

Add the dissolved gelatin to the mango mixture and stir thoroughly.

Pour into a flexible mold with small cube shapes or into a tray to a depth of ⅝ inch (1.5 cm), to be cut later into ¾-inch (2 cm) squares.

Mango Chutney

Finely dice the mango.

Bring the rice vinegar, sugar, and orange juice to a boil.

Reduce the heat and let it reduce to balance the flavors.

Once the syrup cools slightly, stir in the diced mango and allow it to infuse.

Set aside.

Foie Gras, Brioche, *Gelée* and Mango Chutney

Brioche

Cut the brioche slices into ¾-inch (2 cm) squares.

Toast the brioche pieces gently in a frying pan with butter until golden.

Keep dry until serving.

Balsamic Caramel

Pour the balsamic vinegar into a small saucepan and heat over medium heat.

Reduce until it reaches a syrup-like consistency.

Plating

To finish, remove the cheesecloth from the foie gras and slice into ⅜-inch (1 cm) thick rounds with a sharp knife dipped in hot water before each cut.

Slice each round into ¾-inch (2 cm) squares. The trimmings can be used for other presentations.

On a flat plate, create a mosaic by alternating squares of foie gras, brioche, and *gelée*.

Finish with a small spoonful of mango chutney on top of some of the foie gras and brioche squares.

Garnish with the balsamic caramel, apple cut into fine julienne strips, and microgreens.

Herb and Pistachio-Crusted *Carré d'Agneau*, Semolina and Ratatouille

This dish once again reflects the excellence of French cuisine. The rack of lamb is tender and juicy, coated here in a golden, fragrant crust of pistachios and herbs that adds delicious flavor, texture, and aroma. I modified the original recipe by adding pistachios and pairing the couscous with ratatouille, creating an interplay of textures between the fluffiness of the couscous and the silkiness of the vegetables. This accompaniment balances the intensity of the meat and evokes flavors from southern France, especially Nice and Marseille.

4 servings

INGREDIENTS

Carré d'Agneau

- 2 racks of lamb
- 1 c. (100 g) breadcrumbs
- 4 tbsp. (60 g) softened butter
- ¾ oz. (20 g) parsley
- ¼ c. (30 g) shelled pistachios
- 1 garlic clove
- ¼ c. (20 g) grated Parmesan cheese
- Olive oil

Semolina with Ratatouille

- ½ c. (100 g) semolina or couscous
- ⅓ c. + 1 tbsp. (200 ml) chicken stock
- 2 red bell peppers
- 2 zucchini
- 2 eggplants
- 1 red onion
- ⅓ c. + 1 tbsp. (100 ml) vermouth
- Olive oil
- Salt
- Black pepper

Sauce

- ⅓ c. + 1 tbsp. (100 ml) chicken stock
- 1½ tbsp. (20 g) butter

Garnish

- Microgreens

PREPARATION

Carré d'Agneau

Heat 1½ tablespoons (20 g) of butter with a tablespoon of olive oil in a frying pan.

Quickly sear the racks of lamb on all sides and place them in a roasting pan.

Season with salt and pepper.

Prepare the crust by mixing the rest of the butter, the finely chopped parsley, breadcrumbs, grated Parmesan, minced garlic, and finely chopped pistachios.

Using a rolling pin, spread this mixture between 2 sheets of wax paper and chill in the refrigerator.

Cut a rectangle of crust to match the size of the rack of lamb and place on the exterior side of the bone.

Set aside until ready to roast.

Semolina with Ratatouille

Add the semolina to the boiling chicken stock and cover for 30 minutes.

Chop the vegetables into small dice, about ⅛ inch square (3 mm), and sauté each vegetable separately in olive oil.

Make the ratatouille by mixing the sautéed pepper, zucchini, eggplant, and onion in a bowl.

Season with salt and pepper to taste.

Set aside.

Plating

Roast the rack of lamb for 8 minutes at 400 °F (200 °C).

Cut into double chops.

Deglaze the roasting pan with the chicken stock and butter over the stove.

Scrape the bottom of the pan lightly and strain.

Keep warm.

On a plate, spoon the semolina into a ring mold, leaving space in the center using a smaller ring for the ratatouille.

Fill the inner ring with ratatouille, pressing down gently.

Place the rack of lamb next to the semolina and ratatouille.

Chocolate Gratin with Caramelized Pineapple, Praline Cylinder

This dessert plays on contrasting flavors and textures that will surprise any palate. The combination of creamy, deeply flavored, slightly bitter chocolate with the fresh acidity of the caramelized pineapple creates a perfect balance. The praline cylinder provides the finishing touch with its sweetness and crunchy texture, bringing harmony to the creaminess, crunch, and fruitiness of the *gratin*.

4-6 servings

INGREDIENTS

Chocolate Gratin

- 17 oz. (480 g) dark chocolate
- 1 c. (240 ml) whole milk
- ⅔ c. (160 ml) heavy cream
- 6 egg yolks (120 g)
- 16 egg whites (480 g)
- ½ c. + 2 tbsp. (120 g) sugar
- ¼ c. + 1 tsp. (1 oz. / 32 g) cornstarch

Praline

- ½ c. (100 g) sugar
- ⅔ c. (100 g) hazelnuts

Praline Cylinder

- ⅓ c. + 1 tbsp. (100 g) praline (see below)
- 2 oz. (60 g) dark chocolate
- 1½ tbsp. (20 g) cocoa butter
- 1½ c. (50 g) puffed rice cereal
- 2¾ c. (400 g) fresh pineapple
- 1½ tbsp. (20 g) butter
- Honey

Tuile

- ¾ c. + 2 tsp. (100 g) all-purpose flour
- ½ c. (100 g) sugar
- 7 tbsp. (100 g) butter
- 3 egg whites (100 g)

Dark Chocolate Sticks

- 5¼ oz. (150 g) dark couverture chocolate

White Chocolate Half-Cylinder

- 9 oz. (250 g) white couverture chocolate

PREPARATION

Chocolate Gratin

Whisk the egg yolks with the sugar until pale, then add the cornstarch.
Bring the milk and cream to a boil and add the chopped chocolate.
Incorporate the chocolate mixture into the beaten yolks.
Separately, beat the egg whites to soft peaks, gradually adding the sugar.
Gently fold the whites into the chocolate-yolk mixture.
Chill until ready to use.

Praline

Lightly toast the hazelnuts in the oven.
Remove the hazelnuts and rub between your hands to remove the skins.
Prepare a caramel with the sugar, and add the hazelnuts when it starts to brown.
Mix well, spread onto a silicone mat, and let cool.
Blend the mixture into a smooth hazelnut cream.
Set aside.

Praline Cylinder

Melt the chocolate with the cocoa butter and praline, then add the puffed rice.
Spread into the base of a cylindrical mold and chill.

Caramelized Pineapple

Dice the pineapple into small cubes and sauté in butter and honey until soft but not falling apart. Set aside.

Tuile

Melt the butter.
Combine all ingredients in a bowl, then spread the mixture onto a mold in the desired shape.
Bake at 320 °F (160 °C) for 10 minutes.
Unmold carefully.

Chocolate Gratin with Caramelized Pineapple, Praline Cylinder

Chocolate Sticks

Melt the tempered dark chocolate, then spread a thin layer on an acetate sheet.

Let cool slightly.

Cut into sticks measuring ¼ × 4¾ inch (0.5 × 12 cm).

Chill and set aside.

White Chocolate Half-Cylinder

Melt the tempered white chocolate, then spread a thin layer on an acetate sheet.

Let cool slightly.

Cut a rectangle to match the dimensions of the cylinder to be used in assembling the dessert.

Roll the acetate to form a curved shape.

Let cool and set aside.

Plating

Assemble the dessert in layers inside the cylinder mold, starting with the praline base, then the caramelized pineapple, and finally the chocolate mixture.

Gently heat with a kitchen torch and remove the mold.

Wrap the white chocolate half-cylinder around the chocolate gratin, place the chocolate sticks on top, and finish with the *tuile*.

Serve immediately.

m20

- Duck Carpaccio with Hazelnut Oil, Mustard Sauce
- Snapper Fillet with Polenta, Pea Purée, *Mousseline* Sauce
- Walnut-Crusted Venison Medallions, Autumn Purée and Demi-Glace
- Mango Sorbet, Meringue Kisses, Mandarin Gel
- Mascarpone *Mille-Feuille* with Cherries and Blackberry Gel

Chef Jean-Marc Réal

Celebrated for his creativity and understated talent, the French chef Jean-Marc Réal leads the kitchen at his restaurant, Le Saint Martial, located in the village of Saint-Martial de Nabirat. The restaurant features a charming contemporary atmosphere and two small dining rooms warmly and humorously hosted by his wife, Valérie, who recommends wines and describes the dishes. Each dish reflects a deep respect for the ingredients. His cooking is marked by a variety of flavors, cooking techniques, and complementary textures. The couple also prioritizes local ingredients, sourcing them directly from well-known producers throughout France. Jean-Marc Réal brings years of experience in the kitchens of various Relais & Châteaux establishments such as Le Vieux Logis and Château du Breuil, among others.

Duck Carpaccio with Hazelnut Oil, Mustard Sauce

This delicate and elegant carpaccio celebrates the refined flavor of duck with its earthy flavor, which makes it a truly special dish. The toasted, fragrant hazelnut oil enhances the natural silkiness of the duck, adding a warm, slightly sweet note to every bite. The gently emulsified mustard sauce brings brightness and depth. A dish that seduces with its apparent simplicity, while concealing a carefully choreographed interplay of flavors and textures.

4-6 servings

INGREDIENTS

Carpaccio

· 4 duck breasts
· 7 oz. (200 g) arugula
· 2 c. (200 g) shelled walnuts
· ¾ oz. (20 g) radishes
· ½ c. (80 g) red onion
· Hazelnut oil
· Wine vinegar
· 2 tbsp. + 1 tsp. (40 g) salt
· Black pepper

Mustard Sauce

· ⅓ cup (90 g) mayonnaise
· 4 tsp. (20 g) Dijon mustard
· 1 tbsp. (15 g) hazelnut oil
· Salt

PREPARATION

Carpaccio

Trim the duck breasts of excess fat.
Press 2 breasts together, roll tightly in plastic wrap, then wrap in aluminum foil.
Freeze for at least 12 hours.
Remove and finely slice the duck rolls onto a sheet of plastic wrap, forming a rectangle.
Place another sheet of plastic wrap on top, flatten gently, and return to the freezer.
When fully frozen, remove the carpaccio and place on a cutting board.
Using a sharp knife, cut into the desired shape. For this dish, a rectangle.
Measure with a ruler to fit the exact size of the plate.
Lightly toast the walnuts in the oven.
Finely chop and set aside.
Slice the red onion into julienne and set aside.
Finely dice the radishes and set aside.

Mustard Sauce

Combine the mayonnaise and mustard.
Add the oil and salt.
Transfer to a squeeze bottle for the garnish. Set aside

Plating

Lay the carpaccio out on a rectangular serving plate.
Lightly brush with hazelnut oil and season with salt and pepper.
Place the arugula alongside the carpaccio.
Dress with a spoonful of wine vinegar, a splash of hazelnut oil, salt, and pepper.
Garnish with a bit of red onion and a teaspoon of diced radish.
Add several dots of the mustard sauce, and finish with a light dusting of chopped walnuts.
Serve immediately.

Snapper Fillet with Polenta, Pea Purée, *Mousseline* Sauce

Despite its apparent simplicity, this dish harmonizes the subtlety of the sea with gentle vegetable notes. The snapper, with its tender yet firm flesh and naturally sweet flavor, is served with a crisp skin and moist interior. It is accompanied by a soft, lightly toasted polenta that adds warmth and a unique texture. Its mild, comforting character perfectly enhances the nuances of the fish. The pea purée, with its vibrant color and flavor, adds freshness with its sweet herbal notes. Finally, the light and silky *mousseline* sauce coats everything in a refined blend of buttery richness and gentle acidity, adding creaminess while keeping it light.

4 servings

INGREDIENTS

Fish

- 4 skin-on red snapper fillets

Pea Purée

- 2 c. (300 g) green peas or *petit pois*
- ⅓ c. + 1 tbsp. (100 ml) chicken stock
- Salt

Polenta

- 1⅓ c. (250 g) cornmeal (polenta)
- 1¼ c. (300 ml) heavy cream
- 2 c. (500 ml) whole milk
- ½ c. (50 g) grated Parmesan cheese
- 3 eggs

***Mousseline* Sauce**

- 1 c. less 2 tbsp. (200 g) butter
- 3 egg yolks (60 g)
- 1 tbsp. + 1 tsp. (20 ml) lemon juice
- ⅓ c. + 1 tbsp. (100 ml) heavy cream
- Salt

Garnish

- Microgreens

PREPARATION

Pea Purée

Cook the peas in salted water for a few minutes, until tender but still firm.

Remove and cool immediately in ice water to preserve their bright green color.

Blend the peas with 2 tablespoons of chicken stock in a blender. Continue blending, adding more stock only as needed to achieve a smooth, thick purée. Transfer to a piping bag and set aside.

Polenta

Bring the milk and cream to a boil.

Add the cornmeal and stir vigorously for 25 minutes, removing the pot slightly from direct heat.

Remove from the heat and stir in the eggs and Parmesan.

Spread into a mold about 1¼ inch (3 cm) thick and refrigerate. Once firm, cut into the desired shape.

Pan-fry in olive oil until lightly golden.

***Mousseline* Sauce**

Beat the egg yolks with 3 tablespoons of water in a mixing bowl.

Set the bowl over a double boiler.

Continue whisking until the mixture thickens, then remove from the heat.

Melt the butter and add gradually to the yolks, whisking constantly until fully emulsified.

Add the lemon juice and salt to taste. Separately, whip the cream to soft peaks.

Gently fold the whipped cream into the yolk mixture and refrigerate.

Fish

Place the fillets skin-side down in a frying pan with olive oil and sear until the skin is crisp.

Turn the fillets over and cook briefly on the other side. Set aside.

Plating

Arrange the snapper fillet skin-side up on a preheated plate.

Add the sautéed polenta pieces alongside. Pipe a line of pea purée along the length of the fillet and add 2 or 3 dots around it. Garnish the fish and plate with small dots of *mousseline* sauce and microgreens.

Serve immediately.

Walnut-Crusted Venison Medallions, Autumn Purée and Demi-Glace

This dish captures the spirit of the forest and the deep, mellow tones of autumn. The venison medallions, a tender meat with an intense yet refined flavor, are coated in a delicate crust of toasted walnuts that adds a crunchy, earthy note to enhance the game's wild essence. The warm, silky and gently spiced autumn purée offers natural sweetness and a comforting texture that balances the intensity of the meat. The demi-glace, made from a reduction of the venison's own juices, condenses the essence of the game into a dark, glossy and velvety drop that elevates each bite with depth and elegance. If venison is unavailable, the medallions can be replaced with tender cuts of beef filet, lamb, or another mild game.

4 servings

INGREDIENTS

Medallions
- 4 venison medallions
- 5 c. (600 g) walnuts

Demi-Glace Sauce
- Venison bones (from the rib rack)
- 1¼ c. (300 ml) red wine
- ¾ c. + 1 tbsp. (200 ml) beef stock
- ¾ c. (100 g) onion
- ¾ c. (100 g) carrot
- ¾ c. (100 g) celery
- ⅓ c. + 1 tbsp. (50 g) leek
- 1 bay leaf
- 3½ tbsp. (50 g) butter

Autumn Purée
- 2¾ c. (400 g) celery
- 1 apple
- 1 potato
- 1¼ c. (300 ml) whole milk
- 3 tbsp. (40 g) butter
- Heavy cream

Caramelized Endives
- 14 oz. (400 g) endives
- Butter
- Sugar
- Juice of 1 orange

Garnish
- Microgreens and fresh greens

PREPARATION

Demi-Glace Sauce

Marinate the venison bones overnight with the wine, onion, carrots, celery, leek, and bay leaf.
The next day, drain, reserving the marinade, and sear the bones in a hot pan with oil until well browned.
Add the marinated vegetables and brown as well.
Pour in the reserved marinade and beef stock to cover.
Simmer for 2 hours. Strain the sauce and reduce until thick enough to coat the back of a spoon. Set aside.

Medallions

Finely chop the walnuts and coat the sides of the venison medallions, leaving the top and bottom uncovered.

Autumn Purée

Dice the celery, potato, and apples. Simmer the vegetables in milk until soft, then drain.
Blend until smooth, and add the butter.
Stir in a little heavy cream until the purée is soft and creamy. Season to taste. Set aside.

Caramelized Endives

Separate the endive leaves and sauté gently in butter and sugar.
Deglaze with orange juice and reduce. Set aside.

Plating

Sear the venison medallions in oil.
Spoon 1 or 2 tablespoons of purée onto a preheated plate.
Place the venison medallion alongside the purée, overlapping it slightly.
Spoon a bit of the demi-glace around the plate.
Garnish with microgreens and fresh greens.
Serve with the endives, placing 2 leaves on one side of the plate.
Serve immediately.

Mango Sorbet, Meringue Kisses, Mandarin Gel

As the goal was to offer a complete picture of Chef Réal's cuisine without making the menu too heavy, I chose to reinterpret a simple yet delicious dessert. In this refreshing dessert, only the mango sorbet is the chef's original creation; everything else is my inspiration. The mango sorbet is clearly the star of the dish, with its light, velvety texture and sweet, tropical flavor. The mandarin gel, in turn, provides a citrusy contrast with a gelatinous texture that balances the sweetness of the mango. I finished it with meringue kisses, which add a crisp contrast while also bringing a playful element to the dish.

4-6 servings

INGREDIENTS

Mango Sorbet
- 1½ c. (350 g) mango purée
- 1 c. (250 ml) syrup

Syrup
- ⅔ c. (150 ml) water
- ¾ c. (150 g) sugar
- 1 tbsp. (20 g) glucose

Meringue Kisses
- 4 egg whites (125 g)
- 1¼ c. (250 g) sugar

Mandarin Gel
- ¾ c. (175 ml) mandarin juice
- 2 tbsp. (25 g) sugar
- ½ tsp. (2 g) agar-agar

Garnish
- 1 orange
- 1 lime
- 1 grapefruit
- 4 goldenberries or kumquats
- ¾ c. + 1 tbsp. (200 ml) heavy cream
- Fresh mint leaves

PREPARATION

Syrup
Combine all the ingredients in a saucepan.
Bring to a boil and simmer for 1 minute over low heat.
Let cool to room temperature and set aside.

Mango Sorbet
Blend the mango purée with the syrup in a blender.
Strain the mixture and chill in the freezer.
Once thoroughly chilled, churn in an ice cream maker

Meringue Kisses
Combine the egg whites and sugar in a mixing bowl.
Cook over a double boiler, stirring continuously until the sugar dissolves.
Transfer the mixture to the bowl of a stand mixer.
Beat on high speed until stiff peaks form.
Transfer to a piping bag with a plain tip.
Pipe small dots of meringue onto a baking sheet lined with a silicone mat or parchment paper.
For a different presentation, pipe 2 lines of 3 meringues each, touching lightly along their length.
Bake at 185 °F (85 °C) for approximately 2 hours.
Remove from oven and set aside.

Mandarin Gel
Combine all the ingredients in a saucepan.
Bring to a boil, stirring constantly.
Pour into a tray and cover with plastic wrap to prevent a film from forming.
Chill until firm, about 2 hours.
Remove from tray and blend until smooth and glossy.
Transfer to a small squeeze bottle or piping bag.
Set aside.

Mango Sorbet, Meringue Kisses, Mandarin Gel

Garnish

Segment the orange, lime, and grapefruit into supremes.

Slice the goldenberries or kumquats in rounds.

Whip the heavy cream and transfer to a piping bag.

Plating

Arrange the meringue kisses on the plate, alternating with dots of whipped cream.

Add citrus supremes around the plate.

Dot with mandarin gel.

Top with a few slices of goldenberry or kumquat.

Finish with 2 or 3 small scoops of mango sorbet.

Garnish with fresh mint leaves and serve immediately.

For a more original and creative presentation, use the inverted meringue rows as a base.

Arrange the remaining dessert components on top and serve immediately.

Mascarpone *Mille-Feuille* with Cherries and Blackberry Gel

Mille-feuille is a classic French dessert traditionally made with puff pastry and *crème pâtissière*. Chef Réal's original recipe used almond *tuiles* and mascarpone and coffee creams, but I opted for a variation using phyllo dough, known for its extreme thinness and lightness. This allows for a perfect combination between the crunchy texture and the smoothness of the mascarpone filling, enriched by the deep, fruity sweetness of cherries. The blackberry gel, vibrant in both flavor and color, adds a tangy, refreshing touch that brightens the dish and balances the sweetness.

4 servings

INGREDIENTS

Mille-Feuille
- 1 package phyllo dough
- 3½ tbsp. (50 g) butter
- 6 tbsp. (50 g) powdered sugar

Mascarpone Cream
- 2⅔ c. (600 g) mascarpone
- 3⅓ c. (800 g) whipping cream
- 1 tbsp. + 1 tsp. (16 g) gelatin (or 4 sheets)
- 1 vanilla bean
- 10 egg yolks (200 g)
- 1¼ c. (240 g) sugar

Cherries
- 2 c. (300 g) cherries
- ⅓ c. + 1 tbsp. (100 g) water
- ½ c. (100 g) sugar

Blackberry Gel
- ¾ c. (170 g) blackberry juice
- 2 tbsp. + 1 tsp. (30 g) sugar
- ¾ tsp. (2 g) agar-agar

PREPARATION

Mille-Feuille

Roll out the phyllo dough and cut into rectangles of the desired size.
Arrange on a baking tray lined with a silicone mat.
Brush each piece with melted butter and dust with powdered sugar.
Bake at 350 °F (175 °C) for about 10 minutes, or until golden brown.

Mascarpone Cream

Bloom the gelatin sheets in cold water. Remove excess liquid.
Cook the sugar to 250 °F (120 °C) and pour over the egg yolks.
Whisk until light and voluminous.
Add the hydrated gelatin to the warm sabavon. Allow to cool.
Gently fold in the mascarpone and the whipped cream.

Cherries

Heat the water and sugar to make a syrup. Halve and pit the cherries.
Add the cherries to the hot syrup and let them cool in the liquid. Set aside.

Blackberry Gel

Heat the blackberry juice and the sugar.
Add the agar-agar and bring to a boil, stirring constantly.
Pour the mixture into a tray.
Place plastic wrap directly on the surface to prevent a skin from forming.
Chill until set, about 2 hours.
Remove from tray and blend until smooth and glossy.
Transfer to a small squeeze bottle or piping bag. Set aside.

Plating

Assemble the *mille-feuille* starting with a layer of phyllo, followed by mascarpone cream.
Add another layer of phyllo, then blackberry gel, and a final layer of phyllo.
Decorate the top with dots of mascarpone cream and bits of syrup-soaked cherries.

m21

- Mini Arepas, Salmon Roe, with Crème Fraîche
- Pumpkin Tortelloni, Goat Cheese and Honey
- Prawns infused with Curry Aroma
- Lacquered Kid Goat, Creamy Mashed Potatoes, Glazed Carrots
- Chocolate Palet
- *Crema Catalana* Mousse à la Santi
- Petit Fours: *Financiers*, Chocolate Truffle, Meringue Kisses

Chef Santi Santamaria

Widely respected, Catalan chef Santi Santamaria was one of the foremost representatives of Spanish cuisine. The quality of his work was evident in the three Michelin stars earned by his restaurant El Racó de Can Fabes, which he founded in 1994, as well as in the two stars awarded to Santceloni, and the single stars awarded to Evo and Tierra. By 2009, his restaurants had amassed a total of seven Michelin stars. Santamaria was regarded as a passionate advocate for local ingredients and traditional culinary techniques, which he so gracefully captured in the simplicity of his exquisite dishes. Beyond the kitchen, the chef expressed his love for cooking through his books, which remain part of the legacy he left behind before his untimely passing.

Mini Arepas, Salmon Roe, with Crème Fraîche

During his visit to Venezuela, Spanish chef Santi Santamaria had the opportunity to savor and enjoy the cuisine of the country, a place, they say, he held close to his heart. As he liked to say, arepas, *casabe*, and *papelón* were central to the Venezuelan table. He decided to include arepas and several other ingredients in the tasting menu he presented in Caracas. In this particular case, he captured the essence and tradition of Latin American cuisine with a sophisticated and modern touch.

6-8 servings

INGREDIENTS

Arepas

· 5 tbsp. (75 ml) water
· ⅓ c. + 1 tbsp. (50 g) corn flour
· 1 tsp. (5 ml) oil
· Pinch of salt

Filling

· ¾ c. + 1 tbsp. (200 g) crème fraîche or spreadable cream
· 5⅓ oz. (150 g) salmon roe

Garnish

· Microgreens

PREPARATION

Arepas

Combine the warm water with salt and oil in a mixing bowl.
Gradually add the corn flour, stirring continuously.
Knead the dough for a few minutes.
Roll the dough out ⅜ inch (1 cm) thick on a tray lined with a silicone baking mat or parchment paper.
Use a round cutter to form small discs of dough between 1¼ and 1½ inches (3–4 cm) in diameter.
Alternatively, shape the dough into 1¼-inch (3 cm) balls and flatten them to the desired thickness.
Brown the mini arepas on both sides in a frying pan with a little neutral oil until golden.
Remove and cover to keep warm.

Plating

Make a cut lengthwise along the top of the mini arepa.
Fill with cream and add a teaspoon of salmon roe.
Place 2 or 3 mini arepas on a plate.
Garnish with a few microgreens, and serve immediately.

Pumpkin Tortelloni, Goat Cheese and Honey

In the original menu, the chef prepared a pumpkin ravioli which I substituted with tortelloni, a shape that I find more attractive and interesting, yet still a filled pasta. In this preparation, the filling is a soft roasted pumpkin purée, offering a silky texture and natural sweetness that pairs well with the goat cheese cream, which adds complexity and a slight tangy flavor. The dish is finished with the honey and butter mixture, which provides the perfect balance of sweet and savory and coats the tortelloni in a glossy, velvety glaze.

4-6 servings

INGREDIENTS

Pasta
- 1⅔ c. (200 g) 00 flour
- 6 egg yolks
- Corn flour

Filling
- 1 c. (250 g) pumpkin
- ⅓ c. (40 g) Parmigiano Reggiano
- Olive oil
- Salt
- Black pepper

Goat Cheese
- 2 oz. (60 g) goat cheese
- 2 tbsp. (30 ml) heavy cream

Plating and Garnish
- 3½ tbsp. (50 g) honey
- 3 tbsp. (40 g) butter
- Parmigiano Reggiano
- Microgreens
- Edible flowers

PREPARATION

Pasta

Measure the 00 flour into a mixing bowl.

Add the first yolk and begin whisking gently.

Gradually add the remaining yolks, mixing until fully blended.

Turn the dough out onto a floured work surface and knead until you obtain a firm, smooth, and uniform consistency, and no longer sticky.

Wrap the dough in plastic wrap.

Let rest for 30 minutes.

Divide the dough in half and roll it through a pasta machine, starting from the widest setting until it reaches a thickness of 1/16 to 1/12 inch (1–2 mm).

Lay the thin pasta sheets out on a floured surface to prevent sticking.

Use a round cutter to form 2-inch (5 cm) circles from the dough.

Pipe a some pumpkin filling into the center of each round.

Lightly moisten the edge of the circle with a damp fingertip.

Fold in half to form a semicircle, gently pressing the edge to seal.

Bring both corners of the semicircle together and press to form the tortelloni shape.

Place all the tortelloni on a tray lined with parchment paper and a bit of corn flour.

Set aside.

Filling

Peel the pumpkin and dice it into small cubes.

Arrange on a baking sheet.

Drizzle with olive oil and sprinkle with salt.

Roast for 30 minutes at 350 °F (175 °C).

Transfer to a container, add the grated Parmesan, and blend with an immersion blender until smooth and creamy.

Transfer to a piping bag and set aside.

Goat Cheese

Gently heat the heavy cream and mix with the goat cheese until smooth but not runny.

Transfer to a piping bag and set aside.

Pumpkin Tortelloni, Goat Cheese and Honey

Plating

Boil the tortelloni in salted water for a few minutes; they are done when they float to the surface.
In a separate pan, melt the butter and let it begin to brown slightly before adding the honey.
Add a spoonful of the pasta water to emulsify the sauce.
Add the tortelloni and toss gently for 1 minute.
Arrange 5 or 6 tortelloni in a shallow bowl.
Pipe small dots of goat cheese cream and honey-butter glaze.
Garnish with microgreens and edible flower petals.
Serve immediately with finely grated Parmesan.

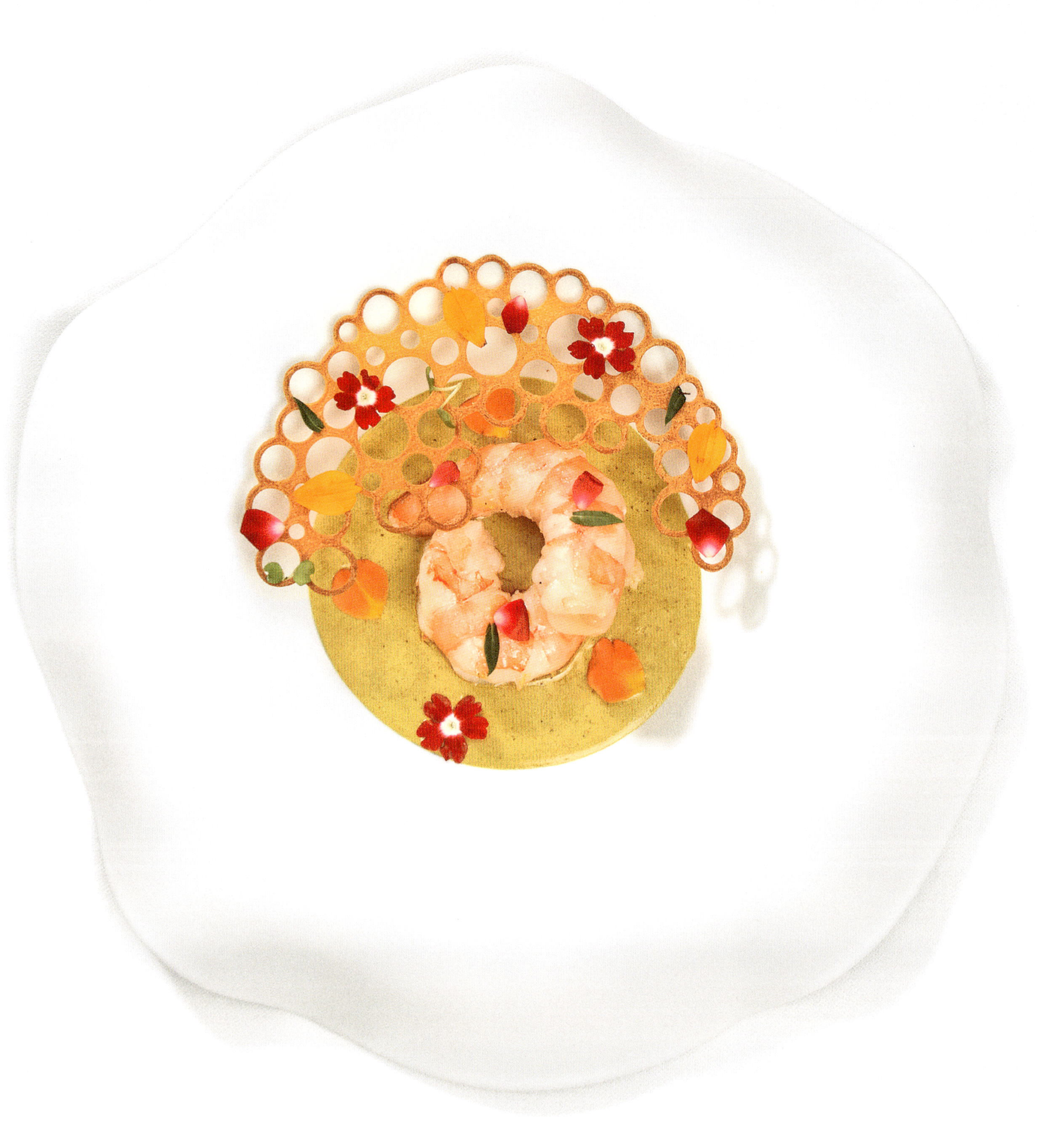

Prawns infused with Curry Aroma

This is a very simple recipe, but one with a unique flavor and aroma. Here I made my version of curry, a recipe adapted from a chef I admire greatly: French chef Eric Ripert. The langoustines are plump and succulent, sweet and delicate in flavor, served with a creamy and spiced curry sauce that gives the dish an aromatic richness.

4-6 servings

INGREDIENTS

Prawns

- 4 to 6 prawns (caliber 16/20)
- Olive oil
- Salt
- Black pepper

Curry Sauce

- 1 c. (240 ml) unsweetened coconut milk
- 2 tbsp. (30 ml) canola oil
- 2 garlic cloves
- 2 to 2½ tsp. (8–10 g) curry powder
- 2 tbsp. (30 g) shallots
- 1 stalk lemongrass
- 1½ tbsp. (20 g) fresh ginger
- Salt
- White pepper

Garnish

- Microgreens
- Edible flowers

PREPARATION

Curry Sauce

Heat the oil in a saucepan.

Finely mince the garlic, shallots, lemongrass, and ginger.

Sauté.

Cook until softened but not browned, about 5 minutes.

Add the curry powder and stir to combine.

Add the coconut milk and let simmer over medium-low heat for 10 minutes.

Remove from heat and strain into another saucepan.

Add salt and freshly ground white pepper to taste.

Set aside.

Prawns

Peel the prawns.

Quickly sauté in olive oil for 3 minutes.

Season with salt and pepper.

Set aside.

Plating

Gently reheat the curry sauce over low heat.

Spoon 1 or 2 tablespoons of the curry sauce into a preheated shallow bowl, enough to coat the bottom.

Place one prawn on top of the sauce.

Garnish with microgreens and edible flower petals.

Serve immediately.

Lacquered Kid Goat, Creamy Mashed Potatoes, Glazed Carrots

Santamaria's lacquered kid goat is a one of those creations that embraces his culinary philosophy: a deep respect for tradition, precise technique, and the use of the highest-quality ingredients. This is a dish that blends modern cooking methods with traditional flavors. The sous-vide cooking method preserves the juiciness of the meat, resulting in a melt-in-your-mouth texture. The dish is finished with a glossy lacquer for a deep golden color. Though the original dish was served with glazed onions, I chose creamy potato purée and glazed carrots to highlight the sweetness of the meat. Both sides pair beautifully with the flavorful kid goat meat.

4-6 servings

INGREDIENTS

Baby Goat

- 1 leg of baby goat
- Olive oil
- Coarse salt
- Whole peppercorns

Lacquer

- 2½ tbsp. (40 g) honey
- 1 tbsp. + 1 tsp. (20 ml) soy sauce
- 1½ tbsp. (20 g) butter

Sauce

- Pan drippings from the goat
- 3 tbsp. (40 g) butter

Potato Purée

- 1 lb. 2 oz. (500 g) potatoes
- 1 c. (250 ml) whole milk
- ½ c. + 1 tbsp. (125 g) butter
- 1 tsp. (5 g) salt

Glazed Carrots

- 1½ c. (200 g) baby carrots
- 3 tbsp. (40 g) butter
- Salt

Garnish

- Microgreens
- Brightly colored flower petals

PREPARATION

Baby Goat

Sear the leg of kid goat in a large frying pan with olive oil.
Transfer to a vacuum bag along with a pinch of coarse salt, whole peppercorns, and a drizzle of olive oil.
Carefully vacuum seal the bag, ensuring no liquid escapes and no air remains inside.
Cook sous vide at 175 °F (80 °C) for 14–16 hours.
Remove and chill immediately in an ice water bath. Set aside.

Lacquer

Melt the butter in a small saucepan.
Add the soy sauce and the honey.
Stir until smooth and fully blended. Set aside.

Potato Purée

Wash the potatoes thoroughly and place in a pot.
Cover with water and bring to a boil.
Once cooked, peel the potatoes and press them through a potato ricer or food mill.
Transfer the puréed potatoes to a pot and reheat, stirring constantly with a spatula.
Add the cold butter cut into small cubes.
Continue stirring and gradually add hot milk until you obtain the desired consistency.
Season with salt.
Transfer to a piping bag and set aside.

Glazed Carrots

Bring a pot of salted water to a boil.
Blanch the carrots for 1 minute.
Drain immediately and let cool.
Slice in half lengthwise, keeping a bit of the stem.

Lacquered Kid Goat, Creamy Mashed Potatoes, Glazed Carrots

Melt the butter in a frying pan.
Add the carrots and glaze for a few minutes until they are al dente and glossy. Set aside.

Sauce
Reheat the bag with the kid goat in the water bath for 15 minutes.
Remove from heat.
Cut open the bag carefully and pour the cooking juices into a pan.
Transfer the meat to a serving platter and cover with foil.
Bring the juices to a boil.
Lower the heat slightly and whisk in the butter to emulsify.
Simmer until the sauce thickens to a silky consistency.

Plating
Place the leg of kid goat on a cutting board and remove the bone.
Cut into 4 to 6 portions.
Brush the lacquer over the kid goat using a pastry brush.
Broil for 2 minutes under a broiler or salamander.
Reheat the sauce thoroughly.
Arrange the piece of kid goat on a preheated plate.
Lay 3 carrots side by side, perpendicular to the meat, with a ¾-inch (2 cm) gap.
Pipe a line of purée between each carrot.
Garnish with microgreens and edible flower petals.
Serve immediately with the hot sauce.

Chocolate Palet

This dessert, which blends refinement with the pure flavor of chocolate, was one of Santi Santamaria's signature dishes. It is a must-try for all chocolate lovers. It delivers an intense chocolate flavor with a smooth, creamy center that balances sweetness and richness beautifully. The orange gel introduces a bright, citrusy counterpoint to the decadent chocolate.

4-6 servings

INGREDIENTS

Chocolate Palet

- 18 oz. (500 g) dark chocolate, 70% cacao
- 2 c. (500 ml) heavy cream
- 3½ tbsp. (50 ml) brandy
- 3½ tbsp. (50 g) butter

Orange Gel

- 1½ c. (375 ml) orange juice
- ½ c. (100 g) sugar
- 2½ tbsp. (35 g) butter
- ½ tsp. (3 g) agar-agar

Garnish

- 9 oz. (250 g) couverture chocolate
- ½ c. (50 g) unsweetened cocoa powder
- Edible flowers

PREPARATION

Chocolate Palet

Finely chop the chocolate.
In a saucepan, bring the cream and brandy to a boil.
Add the chopped chocolate and butter.
Whisk well until the mixture is smooth and fully combined.
Pour into round silicone molds about ½ to ⅝ inch (1-1.5 cm) thick.
Freeze for approximately 3 hours.

Orange Gel

Simmer the orange juice and the sugar in a saucepan until reduced by one-third.
Stir in the butter and cook for another 3 minutes.
Add the agar-agar and bring to a boil, stirring constantly.
Pour into a tray and cover with plastic wrap to prevent a film from forming.
Chill until firm, about 2 hours.
Remove from tray and blend until smooth and glossy.
Transfer to a small squeeze bottle or piping bag.
Set aside.

Garnish

Melt the couverture chocolate.
Pour onto an acetate sheet and spread with a spatula into a ⅟₁₆-inch (2 mm) thick layer.
As the chocolate begins to set, score the surface with a pastry comb.
Roll the acetate sheet and leave until the chocolate is fully set.
Carefully remove the chocolate curls and set aside.

Plating

Unmold the chocolate palet onto a tray.
Dust the palet with cocoa powder and arrange on the serving plate.
Add a few dots of orange gel to one side.
Garnish with chocolate curls and edible flowers.

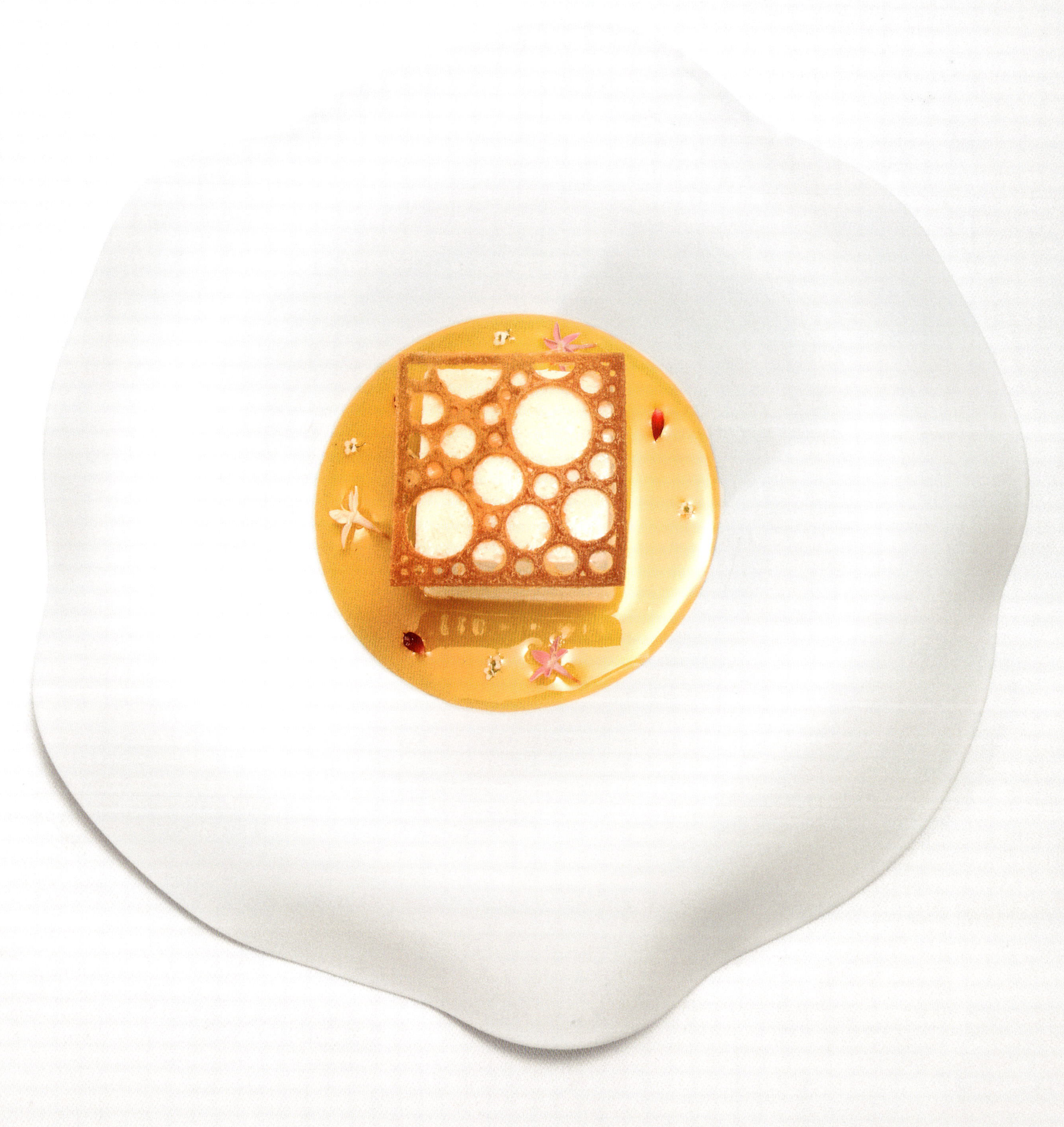

Crema Catalana Mousse à la Santi

This dessert is simply spectacular—a refined reinterpretation of the classic *crema catalana*. The mousse is based on the traditional custard but has a light, airy texture and a clean, elegant look. The orange syrup balances out the mousse's richness and sweetness, while the orange *tuile* adds a delicate crunch and visual finesse.

4-6 servings

INGREDIENTS

Crema Catalana Mousse

- 4¼ c. (1 l) whole milk
- 2 c. (500 ml) heavy cream
- ¾ c. (150 g) sugar
- 6 tbsp. (50 g) cornstarch
- 6 egg yolks (120 g)
- 6 egg whites (180 g)
- 1 tsp. vanilla extract
- 1 piece orange peel
- 5 sheets (14 g) gelatin
- 4¾ tbsp. (70 g) water

Orange _Syrup_

- 4½ c. (1 l) fresh-squeezed orange juice
- 1 c. (200 g) sugar

Orange _Tuile_

- 7 tbsp. (100 g) butter
- ½ c. (100 g) sugar
- 3 egg whites (100 g)
- ¾ c. + 2 tsp. (100 g) all-purpose flour
- Zest of 1 orange

Garnish

- Edible flowers

PREPARATION

Crema Catalana Mousse

Bring the milk to a boil with the orange peel and vanilla.
In a separate bowl, beat the egg yolks with the sugar until pale and doubled in volume.
Slowly add the hot milk to the yolk mixture, whisking continuously.
Add the cornstarch and return to the heat, stirring continuously until thickened.
Add the previously bloomed and melted gelatin sheets.
Let cool to room temperature.
In a separate bowl, beat the egg whites to soft peaks and fold them into the mixture.
Whip the heavy cream until it holds stiff peaks, then fold into the mixture.
Pour the mousse into 1½-inch (4 cm) square silicone molds, or whichever shape mold you prefer.
Smooth the surface with a spatula and freeze for at least 24 hours.

Orange Syrup

Combine the orange juice and sugar in a small saucepan.
Simmer over low heat until reduced by half.

Orange _Tuile_

Preheat the oven to 350 °F (175 °C).
Gently melt the butter, without letting it brown.
Combine the flour, sugar, orange zest, and egg whites, then add the melted butter.
Mix until smooth.
Spread a thin layer of the batter onto a silicone *tuile* mold, smoothing with a spatula for clean edges.
Bake for 4–6 minutes or until golden and easily released from the mold.
Gently lift the *tuile* from the mold and allow it to cool completely.

Plating

Unmold the mousse into a shallow bowl.
Let thaw for about 20 minutes.
Spoon the orange syrup around the mousse.
Place the *tuile* directly on top.
Garnish with a few edible flower petals.
Serve immediately.

Petit Fours: *Financiers*, Chocolate Truffle, Meringue Kisses

No great menu should end without petit fours, which offer a bite-sized burst of flavor and finesse. Here I've included a few timeless favorites. The *financiers*, French almond-based tea cakes, were made in square molds instead of the usual rectangular ones, perfect for a single bite. They're slightly crisp on the outside and moist and tender inside. I also included the chocolate truffle, a true culinary classic. Made with a rich, creamy ganache flavored with brandy and rolled in cocoa powder, the truffle melts in your mouth with a deep, complex chocolate flavor. Finally, the meringue kisses—sweet, crisp clouds that melt on the palate—bring an additional texture to these petit fours.

Financiers

6-8 servings

INGREDIENTS

- 1 c. + 2 tbsp. (250 g) butter
- 7 egg whites (200 g)
- 1⅔ c. (200 g) powdered sugar
- ⅔ c. (80 g) all-purpose flour
- ¾ c. (80 g) almond flour

PREPARATION

Melt the butter in a saucepan and continue cooking until it turns a golden brown.
Strain and set aside.
Beat the egg whites until soft peaks form.
While continuing to beat, slowly add the powdered sugar until fully combined.
Gently fold in the all-purpose flour and the almond flour.
Stir in the melted butter until fully combined.
Cover the mixture with plastic wrap.
Refrigerate overnight.
Remove from the fridge and transfer the batter to a piping bag.
Grease a silicone *financier* mold with butter. If using a metal mold, also dust with flour.
Fill the mold(s) three-quarters full.
Bake at 350 °F (175 °C) for 8–10 minutes.
Remove from the oven and let cool before unmolding.

Chocolate Truffle

12 servings

INGREDIENTS

- 18 oz. (500 g) dark chocolate
- 1¼ c. (300 ml) heavy cream
- 3½ tbsp. (50 g) butter
- 3½ tbsp. (50 ml) brandy
- Cocoa powder to dust

PREPARATION

Finely chop the chocolate and combine in a mixing bowl with the butter.
Bring the cream and brandy to a boil in a saucepan.
Pour the hot mixture over the chocolate and butter, stirring until smooth and fully blended.
While still liquid, pour into sphere-shaped silicone molds.
Freeze for 2 hours or until firm.
If you don't have a sphere mold, pour the mixture into a glass dish and freeze for 1 hour.
Once partially firm, scoop out small balls using a parisienne scoop.
Place the truffles on a tray and freeze again until firm.
As soon as they have set, dust with cocoa powder.
They can be stored covered in the fridge.
Let them come to room temperature for 10–15 minutes before serving.

Meringue Kisses

12 servings

INGREDIENTS

· 4 egg whites (125 g)
· 1¼ c. (250 g) sugar

PREPARATION

Combine the egg whites and sugar in a mixing bowl.
Cook over a double boiler, stirring continuously until the sugar dissolves.
Transfer the mixture to the bowl of a stand mixer and beat at high speed until stiff peaks form.
Fill a piping bag with a plain tip.
Pipe small dots of meringue onto a baking sheet lined with a silicone mat or parchment paper.
For a different presentation, pipe 2 lines of 3 meringues each, touching lightly along their length.
Bake at 185 °F (85 °C) for approximately 2 hours.
Remove from oven and set aside.

Petit Fours: *Financiers*, Chocolate Truffle, Meringue Kisses

Plating

For the plating, I used a charming ring-shaped dish. The idea is to combine different petit fours on a plate that is elegant and eye-catching, reflecting the delicacy of these treats. For this version, I arranged two *financiers*, two meringue kisses, and three truffles, alternating with edible flowers, dots of orange gel, and dabs of chocolate ganache.

m22

- *Cozze al Pomodoro*
- *Rigatoni ai Quattro Formaggi*
- *Agnello Cacio e Ova*
- *Panna Cotta,* Blackberry Coulis

Chef Fabio Serra

The Italian chef Fabio Serra is originally from Villa Santa Maria, in Abruzzo, a town internationally recognized as the homeland of Italian chefs. It is home to the Istituto Alberghiero Villa Santa Maria, a renowned hospitality school founded in 1939, where Serra worked as a professor. In 2008, he traveled to Venezuela under a program led by the Italian Trade Institute of the Italian Embassy, offering Italian cooking courses. He has returned to the country several times and is well known for his appearances on television, where he performs live cooking demonstrations, showcasing his passion for Italian cuisine.

Cozze al Pomodoro

This is a delicious, easy-to-make recipe that captures the flavors of the sea and the freshness of ripe tomatoes. The mussels are gently steamed to highlight their delicate briny taste. They are served with a smooth, velvety tomato sauce that perfectly balances the mussels and their juices and the intensity of the tomato flavor. Accompany with toasted ciabatta slices or any other bread, such as baguette or rustic bread.

4-6 servings

INGREDIENTS

Tomato Sauce

- 1 c. (250 g) San Marzano peeled tomatoes
- 4 garlic cloves
- 1 tbsp. (15 g) salt
- 2 tsp. (10 g) sugar

Mussels

- 4½ lbs. (2 kg) fresh mussels
- ¾ c. + 1 tbsp. (200 ml) white wine
- ¾ c. (100 g) onion
- 2 garlic cloves
- Olive oil
- Salt
- Black pepper

Garnish

- Microgreens
- Edible flower petals

PREPARATION

Tomato Sauce

Heat enough olive oil in a deep saucepan to cover the bottom.
Add the peeled garlic cloves to infuse the oil.
Tilt and swirl the pot so the garlic turns a deep golden brown, but doesn't burn.
Remove the garlic and leave the oil in the pot.
Carefully add the tomatoes to the oil over medium heat. Bring to a boil.
Stir with a wooden spoon, crushing the tomatoes as you stir.
Once the sauce begins to boil, add the salt and sugar.
Simmer over low heat for 1 hour.
Remove from heat and purée the sauce.
Adjust salt to taste.
Keep warm and set aside.

Mussels

Rinse the mussels thoroughly and chill until needed.
In a pot, sauté the finely diced onion in olive oil for 3 to 4 minutes.
Add the chopped garlic and cook for 1 more minute.
Add the white wine and bring to a boil.
Immediately add the mussels, cover and steam for 6 to 7 minutes or until they open, stirring two or three times.
Remove from heat and discard any unopened mussels.
Set aside.

Plating

Spoon a generous amount of hot tomato sauce into a preheated bowl or deep plate.
Arrange 6 or 7 mussels on top, facing different angles.
Garnish with microgreens and edible flower petals.
Serve immediately.

Rigatoni ai Quattro Formaggi

Rigatoni with four-cheese sauce is a feast of textures and flavors. This pasta, with its characteristic cylindrical, ridged shape, holds the creamy sauce perfectly, with each rigatoni coated in a silky layer of melted cheeses. In this version, I've opted for a more playful presentation, arranging the pasta on top of the sauce instead of covering it completely, and serving extra warmed sauce on the side.

4 servings

INGREDIENTS

Rigatoni ai Quattro Formaggi

- 14 oz. (400 g) rigatoni
- 3½ oz. (100 g) Gorgonzola cheese
- 3½ oz. (100 g) Fontina cheese
- 3½ oz. (100 g) Taleggio cheese
- 5¼ oz. (150 g) Grana Padano cheese
- 1 c. heavy cream
- 7 tbsp. (100 g) butter
- Salt
- Black pepper

Garnish

- Microgreens
- Edible flower petals

PREPARATION

Rigatoni ai Quattro Formaggi

Crumble the Gorgonzola, Fontina, and Taleggio, and grate half of the Grana Padano.
Combine the cheeses in a wide frying pan with the butter, a pinch of salt, and pepper.
Add the cream once the cheeses have fully melted.
Keep warm.
Bring a large pot of salted water to a boil.
Add the pasta and cook.
Drain pasta once it is al dente.

Plating

Spoon a bit of cheese sauce into a shallow bowl.
Arrange 6 or 7 rigatoni at different angles on top.
Garnish with microgreens and flower petals.
Sprinkle with grated Grana Padano and serve immediately.
A simpler serving option is to toss the al dente pasta directly in the pan with the cheese.
Heat through for 1–2 minutes.
Serve a ladleful of pasta on each plate.
Add the remaining grated Grana Padano.
Garnish with microgreens and edible flower petals.
Serve immediately.

Agnello Cacio e Ova

This dish, a traditional specialty from the Abruzzo region, celebrates bold, rustic flavors in a refined, modern presentation. The lamb is slowly braised until tender and juicy. The sauce that gives the dish its name is a carefully refined blend of cheese and eggs, resulting in a silky texture. Finally, the tenderness of the meat pairs in perfect harmony with the salty, gently tangy character of the pecorino, yielding a dish that is simply exquisite

4 servings

INGREDIENTS

Lamb
- 1 lb. 2 oz. (500 g) lamb
- 2 c. (500 ml) vegetable broth
- 1 c. (120 g) all-purpose flour
- ¾ c. (100 g) onion
- ⅓ c. + 1 tbsp. (100 ml) dry white wine
- 1½ tbsp. (20 ml) olive oil
- Nutmeg
- Salt

Sauce
- ½ c. (60 g) grated pecorino cheese
- 2 eggs
- 2 lemons

Carrot Purée
- 2 c. (300 g) carrots
- ⅓ c. + 1 tbsp. (100 ml) chicken broth

***Tuile* Crisp**
- 3½ tbsp. (50 g) butter
- ½ c. (50 g) all-purpose flour
- 2 egg whites (50 g)
- ⅛ tsp. (0.5 g) salt

Garnish
- Microgreens
- Edible flower petals

PREPARATION

Lamb

Slice the onion into julienne strips and sauté gently in olive oil.

Season with a pinch of nutmeg and continue to cook over low heat.

Dice the lamb into ¾ × 1¼-inch (2 × 3 cm) pieces. Dredge the lamb pieces in flour.

Add the lamb to the pot and sauté with the onion. Cook over low heat.

Add a pinch of salt, then deglaze with white wine.

Once the wine has evaporated, pour in the vegetable broth.

Simmer gently for about 2 hours. Remove the meat and place it on a tray. Cover and set aside.

Sauce

In a bowl, combine the beaten eggs with the lemon juice and grated pecorino.

Pour the egg and cheese mixture into the cooking liquid left in the pot.

Stir vigorously to blend all the ingredients. Strain the sauce and heat gently. Set aside.

Carrot Purée

Slice the carrots into rounds and add to a saucepan.

Cover with the chicken stock and simmer over medium heat.

Once the carrots are tender, blend at high speed for 2 minutes with as little liquid as possible until silky and glossy. Add the butter and blend again. Season with salt.

Transfer to a squeeze bottle and set aside.

***Tuile* Crisp**

Combine all ingredients.

Spread the mixture in a *tuile* mold into the desired shape.

Bake in a preheated oven at 350 °F (175 °C) for 5 minutes.

Plating

On a preheated plate, make 2 shapes with the carrot purée—1 large, 1 small.

Carefully spoon some of the sauce into each shape outline.

Place 2 or 3 pieces of lamb in the large shape and 1 in the smaller one.

Place a *tuile* on top of the lamb and drizzle with olive oil. Garnish with microgreens and edible flower petals. Serve immediately.

Panna Cotta, Blackberry Coulis

This traditional Italian dessert could not be absent from this menu. It is characterized by its velvety texture and delicate balance of flavors. Here I present it unmolded, with a smooth, glossy surface and a minimalist touch that highlights its purity. *Panna cotta* pairs wonderfully with acidic fruit coulis—in this case blackberry—which provides an intense contrast. Alternatively, it can be served with melted chocolate or caramel, both of which enhance its creamy flavor.

4-6 servings

INGREDIENTS

Panna Cotta

- 1⅔ c. (400 ml) heavy cream
- ⅔ c. (150 ml) whole milk
- ¼ c. + 1 tbsp. (60 g) sugar
- 2½ sheets gelatin
- 1 vanilla bean

Blackberry Coulis

- 1 c. (150 g) blackberries
- ¼ c. + 2 tbsp. (75 g) sugar
- 3½ tbsp. (50 ml) water

Garnish

- Edible flower petals

PREPARATION

Panna Cotta

In a saucepan, heat the cream and milk with the sugar and vanilla.
Bring to a boil.
Remove from heat.
Discard the vanilla bean.
Add the gelatin sheets, previously bloomed in cold water.
Mix well and pour into silicone molds of the desired shape.
Chill until set.
Once firm, transfer the molds to the freezer for at least 4 hours.
Remove from the freezer and unmold 2 hours before serving.
Chill in the refrigerator until ready to use.

Blackberry Coulis

Bring the blackberries and the water to a boil in a small saucepan.
Strain through a fine sieve to extract all the pulp.
Return the liquid to the pot and heat with the sugar.
Simmer over low heat until it reaches a syrup-like consistency.

Plating

Spoon the blackberry coulis into a shallow bowl to cover the base.
Gently set the *panna cotta* on top of the coulis.
Garnish with different flower petals.
Serve immediately.

m23

- Gazpacho with its Frozen Sphere, Fresh Goat Cheese, Toasted Baguette
- Malanga *Mousseline* Ravioli, Mushrooms and Cream Sauce
- Quail with Braised Cabbage, Cashews, Baby Potatoes, and Pearl Onions in *Sauce Périgueux*
- Caramelized Crêpe Soufflé, Passion Fruit Sauce

Chef Claude Troisgros

Chef Claude Troisgros was born in Roanne, France in 1955, into a family with a rich multinational-generational culinary heritage. He began his career at Les Frères Troisgros, the restaurant founded by his father and uncle, pioneers of the *nouvelle cuisine* movement in France. He later moved to Brazil to open his own restaurant, Olympe, in Rio de Janeiro, where he fused French techniques with Brazilian ingredients. Troisgros has also appeared on television shows and authored several cookbooks. He is regarded as one of Brazil's most influential chefs and has received numerous awards and honors.

Gazpacho with its Frozen Sphere, Fresh Goat Cheese, Toasted Baguette

This dish is a refreshing and surprising reinterpretation of the classic Andalusian gazpacho. The liquid base preserves the vibrant essence of ripe tomatoes, enhanced with a touch of olive oil. This cold soup, perfect for summer, plays with temperature, texture, and tradition, but with a modern twist. The frozen gazpacho sphere is the unexpected star of the dish. As it melts, it releases a wave of icy freshness, intensifying the experience and adding a unique texture between sorbet and cold soup. To the side, a thin, crisp slice of golden toasted bread adds a rustic and satisfying note. A creamy dollop of fresh goat cheese adds a soft dairy note with character, balancing the acidity of the gazpacho with finesse.

4 servings

INGREDIENTS

Gazpacho

- 2 lb. 3 oz. (1 kg) ripe tomatoes
- ½ c. (70 g) peeled cucumber
- ¼ c. (40 g) onion
- 2 garlic cloves
- ½ tbsp. tomato paste
- 2 tbsp. (30 ml) red wine vinegar
- ¼ c. (60 ml) olive oil
- Salt

Cream Cheese

- 14 oz. (400 g) fresh goat cheese
- 2 tbsp. heavy cream
- 2 baguettes
- 4 tbsp. extra virgin olive oil
- 12 cherry tomatoes

Garnish

- Basil microgreens

PREPARATION

Gazpacho

Chop the tomatoes, cucumber, and onion.

Combine all the ingredients for the gazpacho and let them marinate for 1 hour.

Transfer to a blender and process at high speed until completely smooth.

Strain and adjust salt to taste if necessary.

Pour a small amount of the gazpacho into flexible half-sphere molds or, alternatively, into different sized measuring spoons.

Freeze.

Refrigerate the remaining gazpacho.

Goat Cream Cheese

Blend the goat cheese with the 2 tablespoons of cream until smooth.

Transfer to a squeeze bottle or piping bag, and set aside.

Toasted Baguette

Cut the baguette into 6-inch (15 cm) long slices, about ⅛ inch (3 mm) thick.

Arrange on a baking sheet and drizzle with olive oil.

Place another tray on top to keep the bread flat while toasting.

Bake for a few minutes until golden.

Once toasted, pipe small dollops of the goat cream cheese on the bread, alternating with quartered cherry tomatoes.

Plating

Spoon a bit of gazpacho into a chilled bowl.

Place 2 frozen gazpacho spheres in the soup.

Drizzle in a few drops of olive oil.

Finish by resting the piece of toasted bread with cheese and tomato across the edge of the bowl.
Garnish with basil microgreens.

Serve immediately.

Malanga *Mousseline* Ravioli, with Mushrooms and Cream Sauce

A delicate, comforting recipe that reimagines tradition from a creative angle. These ravioli, made with fine wonton wrappers instead of traditional pasta, offer a silky, light texture that gently envelopes the filling. Inside, a *mousseline* made with malanga—a tropical root known for its delicate flavor and creamy, soft, airy consistency, blends with the earthy intensity of the mushrooms, creating a contrast between natural sweetness and deep umami. The creaminess of the sauce rounds out the dish with richness, bringing all the elements together with warmth and elegance.

4 servings

INGREDIENTS

Ravioli

- ¾ c. (200 g) malanga root (taro)
- ¼ c. (60 ml) heavy cream
- 1 tbsp. (15 ml) white truffle oil (or extra virgin olive oil)
- 24 wonton wrappers
- Salt
- Black pepper

Sauce

- 1 tbsp. mushroom *glacé* (or chicken stock concentrate)
- 2 c. (500 ml) heavy cream
- Salt
- Black pepper

Mixed Mushrooms

- 1 c. (100 g) chanterelle
- 1 c. (100 g) shiitake
- 1 c. (100 g) shimeji
- 2 c. (200 g) white button
- 1 c. (100 g) portobello

PREPARATION

Malanga *Mousseline*

Peel and dice the malanga root into ⅝-inch (1.5 cm) cubes.
Cook in salted water for 40 minutes.
While still hot, purée with an immersion blender until smooth.
Bring the heavy cream to a boil and combine with the malanga purée.
Add salt and pepper to taste.
Strain through a fine mesh sieve and blend once more in a food processor. Set aside.

Ravioli

Spoon 1 tablespoon of the *mousseline* onto a wonton wrapper.
Moisten the edges and place a second wrapper on top.
Seal and cut into the desired shape using a ravioli cutter.
Cook in salted water with a dash of oil for easier handling.
Remove immediately and place on a lightly oiled tray.

Mushrooms

Gently clean the mushrooms with a damp paper towel.
Slice the button and portobello mushrooms into 1⁄16-inch (2 mm) slices.
Sauté all the mushrooms in butter. Season with salt and pepper.

Sauce

Deglaze the mushroom pan with the mushroom *glacé*.
Stir in the cream and bring to a boil.
Season with salt and pepper. Whisk until smooth.

Plating

Spoon some sauce onto a preheated plate.
Arrange 3 raviolis on top of the sauce.
Top each raviolo with some sautéed mushrooms.
Finish with a few drops of truffle oil.
Garnish with a microgreen, and serve immediately.

Quail with Braised Cabbage, Cashews, Baby Potatoes, and Pearl Onions in *Sauce Périgueux*

This dish combines delicacy with bold character. The original Troisgros recipe was a quail stuffed with foie gras and *farofa* (a Brazilian preparation made with yuca flour). In this version, I created a deconstructed take on the dish, where the quail—with its tender meat and elegant flavor—is presented in golden, juicy pieces alongside slowly braised cabbage for sweet, rich notes. Finely chopped cashew nuts add crunch and a hint of toasted flavor that contrasts with the softness of the potatoes and onions, adding both volume and rustic charm to the composition. The *sauce Périgueux*, a French classic, envelops the dish with its earthy, refined aroma, enhancing each element with intensity and sophistication. Altogether, it's an autumnal harmony of textures and deep flavor, where each ingredient blends seamlessly with the next.

4 servings

INGREDIENTS

Quail
- 2 quail
- 3½ tbsp. (50 g) butter
- 3 tbsp. (40 g) duck fat
- Salt
- Black pepper

Vegetables
- 1 medium cabbage
- 8 cashew nuts
- 8 baby potatoes
- 8 pearl onions
- 1 c. chicken broth
- 1 onion
- 4 garlic cloves
- Salt
- Black pepper

Sauce
- Quail carcasses
- 1⅓ c. (200 g) carrots
- 1⅓ c. (200 g) onion
- ¾ c. (100 g) celery
- ⅓ c. (50 g) shallots
- 2 garlic cloves
- ⅓ c. + 1 tbsp. (100 ml) Madeira or Port wine
- 2 c. (500 ml) chicken broth
- 7 tbsp. (100 g) butter
- 2 slices foie gras pâté (1½–1¾ oz. / 40–50 g total)
- 1 tbsp. (20 g) black truffle

PREPARATION

Quail

Remove both quail legs carefully, keeping the skin intact.

Detach the breasts from the bone and divide each in half.

Save the skin and reserve the carcass with leftover meat for the sauce base.

Lightly salt and pepper both the legs and breasts.

Brown them skin-side down in duck fat or butter until crisp and golden.

Flip gently and cook a little longer.

Remove from heat and set aside.

Sauce

Roast the quail carcasses with 1½ tablespoons (20 g) of butter in a roasting tray at 350 °F (175 °C) until browned, about 15–20 minutes.

Deglaze the pan with the Madeira wine.

Allow to reduce, then stir in 2 tablespoons of stock and transfer everything to a pot.

Add the carrots, onion, celery, garlic, and just enough chicken stock to barely cover the bones.

Simmer over medium heat for 1 hour.

Strain and simmer again until reduced by half.

Whisk in 6 tablespoons (80 g) of cold butter, cubed.

Once emulsified, melt in the foie gras slices.

Strain again through a fine sieve, add the finely diced black truffle, and set aside.

Vegetables

Blanch the cabbage and cut into julienne strips.

Sauté the chopped onion and garlic.

Add the cabbage and sauté a bit longer.

Deglaze with chicken stock and reduce until dry.

Quail with Braised Cabbage, Cashews, Baby Potatoes, and Pearl Onions in *Sauce Périgueux*

Season to taste.
Parboil the baby potatoes and then sauté in butter.
Sauté the pearl onions in butter until brown and caramelized.
Toast the cashews and chop finely.
Set each vegetable aside separately.

Plating
Heat a bit of butter in a pan until it turns golden brown.
Reheat the quail pieces skin-side down for a few minutes.
Arrange a quail breast and leg on a large, preheated plate.
Add a spoonful of cabbage and sprinkle with chopped cashews.
Add some baby potatoes and glazed onions.
Spoon over the sauce.
Garnish with microgreens.

Caramelized Crêpe Soufflé, Passion Fruit Sauce

This recipe, based on one of the chef's signature desserts, is reimagined in a lighter, more modern and manageable format. It's an elevated twist on the classic French crêpe. A crepe shuffle that surprises with its lightness and ethereal texture. The base is an airy batter of whipped egg whites that gently puffs up into an almost heavenly fluffiness. The caramelized surface adds a golden, crisp contrast reminiscent of crème brûlée, bringing depth and a delicate bitterness. The passion fruit sauce, intense, tangy, and fragrant, delivers a burst of tropical freshness that balances the overall sweetness, infusing each bite with its exotic and vibrant character.

4 servings

INGREDIENTS

Pastry Cream
- 6 egg yolks
- ¾ c. (150 g) sugar
- ¾ c. (100 g) cornstarch
- 2 c. (475 ml) milk
- 1 vanilla bean

Crêpe
- 2 c. (475 ml) milk
- 6 tbsp. (85 g) butter
- 8 egg yolks
- ⅔ c. (80 g) all-purpose flour
- ½ tsp. salt
- 8 egg whites
- ¾ c. + 2 tbsp. (170 g) sugar
- Pinch of salt

Passion Fruit Sauce
- ½ c. + 1 tbsp. (120 g) sugar
- 3½ tbsp. (50 ml) water
- ½ c. (120 g) cold butter
- ½ c. (125 ml) seedless passion fruit pulp
- Powdered sugar for caramelizing

Tuile
- 7 tbsp. (100 g) butter
- ½ c. (100 g) sugar
- 3 egg whites (100 g)
- ¾ c. (100 g) all-purpose flour

Garnish
- Edible flowers
- *Tuile*

PREPARATION

Pastry Cream

Whisk the egg yolks and sugar together until pale and smooth.
Add the cornstarch and continue whisking until fully combined.
Place the milk in a saucepan.
Split the vanilla pod, scrape out the seeds, and add them to the milk.
Bring to a boil.
Pour a spoonful of hot milk into the yolk mixture, stir to combine, and then add the remaining milk.
Cook over medium heat, stirring constantly, until the mixture thickens and starts to bubble.
Remove from heat and transfer to a clean mixing bowl.
Cover with plastic wrap, pressing it against the surface to prevent a skin from forming.
Refrigerate for a minimum of 2 hours.
When fully chilled, transfer to a piping bag.

Crêpe

Whisk the egg yolks and sugar together until pale and light.
Add the flour and mix until fully combined.
Heat the milk with the butter.
In a separate bowl, whisk the egg whites with a pinch of salt, gradually adding the sugar.
Continue whisking until soft peaks form.
Slowly add the hot milk to the yolk mixture, whisking continuously until fully combined.
Gently fold the meringue into the yolk mixture as you would do for a soufflé.
Heat a nonstick pan and grease with butter.
Place 2-inch (4–5 cm) rings in the pan and pour the batter to ¾-inch (2 cm) height.
Cook 2–3 minutes until the base is golden.
Flip and cook for 2 more minutes until golden on the other side.

Caramelized Crêpe Soufflé, Passion Fruit Sauce

Remove from the pan and cool on a wooden cutting board.

Carefully remove the crêpe from the mold and slice in half horizontally.

Fill with a spoonful of pastry cream.

Set aside.

Passion Fruit Sauce

Heat the passion fruit pulp.

Once heated, pulse twice with an immersion blender.

Strain and set aside.

Combine the sugar and water in a small saucepan.

Cook on high until the mixture turns a pale caramel color.

Stir in the strained pulp.

Bring the mixture to a boil.

Reduce heat to medium-low and simmer for 5 minutes.

Add the butter and remove from heat.

Set aside.

Tuile

Preheat the oven to 350 °F (175 °C).

Gently melt the butter.

Combine the flour, sugar, and egg whites, then add the melted butter.

Mix until smooth.

Spread a thin layer of the batter onto a silicone *tuile* mold, smoothing with a spatula for clean edges.

Bake for 4–6 minutes or until golden and easily released from the mold.

Gently lift the *tuile* to avoid breakage.

Allow to cool.

Plating

Sprinkle the crêpes with powdered sugar.

Use a kitchen torch to caramelize the surface of each crêpe.

Spoon some passion fruit sauce into a shallow bowl.

Place a filled crêpe on top of the sauce.

Garnish with *tuile* and edible flower petals.

Serve immediately.

Published by
TURNER

Editorial Coordination
Laura Estévez / Turner

Texts
Brigitte Dolman

Copyediting
Laura Badsey / Turner

Proofreading
Miryana Márquez

Photographs
Julio Osorio

Photographic Retouching
Gady Alroy / ArtMedia Studio

Graphic Design
Raúl Lira / Studio Design
Juanita Antonorsi / Studio Design

Production
Enol Álvarez / Turner

Distribution
Turner

ISBN: 978-84-19539-31-1
Legal Deposit: M-18978-2025
Printed in Spain

Our distributors are essential for our books to reach their readers. On this journey, we are joined by Machado in Spain, Océano in Latin America, DAP in the United States and Canada, and Central Books in Europe.